Pharmaceutical Supply Chain

Drug Quality and Security Act

Pharmaceutical Supply Chain

Drug Quality and Security Act

Fred A. Kuglin

CRC Press
Taylor & Francis Group
Boca Raton London New York

CRC Press is an imprint of the
Taylor & Francis Group, an **informa** business

CRC Press
Taylor & Francis Group
6000 Broken Sound Parkway NW, Suite 300
Boca Raton, FL 33487-2742

First issued in paperback 2021

© 2016 by Taylor & Francis Group, LLC
CRC Press is an imprint of Taylor & Francis Group, an Informa business

No claim to original U.S. Government works

ISBN-13: 978-1-4822-5893-6 (hbk)
ISBN-13: 978-1-03-217969-8 (pbk)
DOI: 10.1201/b18697

Visit the Taylor & Francis Web site at
http://www.taylorandfrancis.com

and the CRC Press Web site at
http://www.crcpress.com

Contents

Preface

This book looks at the Drug Quality and Security Act of 2013 and how it will potentially impact the supply chain participants and professionals throughout the pharmaceutical drug supply chain. Several of the provisions in this act were not yet finalized by the press time of this book, but the direction of the overall act has been set by Congress and signed into law by the president of the United States.

My focus as a supply chain practitioner, first within industry and later in consulting, has always been end-to-end anchored by the patient/consumer. Little did I know that the origins for this book would begin with me as a consumer in sixth grade. I was riding my bicycle on the sidewalk when someone called out to me. I looked back, and the next thing I knew, I woke up on the couch with a doctor (back when doctors still made house calls) beside me. My friends said that when I looked back, I veered off the sidewalk and hit a tree, knocking me out. I had a lot of cuts, so the doctor gave me a penicillin shot. My body reacted with Stevens–Johnson syndrome, a rare, serious disorder of the skin and mucous membranes. I was in a coma for two weeks. Stevens–Johnson syndrome requires hospitalization and can be life threatening. It is usually a reaction to a medication or an infection, with treatment focusing on eliminating the underlying cause. In my case, this meant not ever taking penicillin or "cillin"-based antibiotics again.

Since then, I have been uber-cautious about taking any pharmaceutical drugs. I have also been intrigued with both drug quality and drug safety, knowing the downsides firsthand. In 2007–2008, I had the pleasure of working on ePedigree solutions with a group anchored by supply chain and authentication companies. It became evident to me that pharmaceutical drug diversion, substitution, and in some cases, quality control were issues that were bigger than the general public realized. Not much can be done when a body (like mine) decides to have a reaction to a specific drug. We see the disclaimers all the time in pharmaceutical drug advertising. Usually the tolerance is around 1–3% of all patients/consumers. This happens because, as humans, each of our bodies is unique. However, what I did learn is that we must collectively do everything we can within our power to avoid external forces manipulating or tampering with pharmaceutical drugs or purposely ignoring current good manufacturing practices that needlessly endanger patients/consumers. When failures in these areas occur, people get sick, can become disabled, and in select cases, die as a result.

In 2011–2012, I had the pleasure of working with a few companies that volunteered to send excess medical equipment and pharmaceutical drugs to developing countries. One individual had been a third-generation owner of a small medical device manufacturer. Despite having a stellar safety record, the cost of regulation caused him to close down his company. His family still owns the patent on the medical device. No other company stepped up to produce the device and utilize his patent. All the patients/consumers who could benefit from this device are now doing without because of excess regulation.

When the opportunity came for me to write this book, I was intrigued for a couple of reasons. First, I had just had neck surgery, directly benefiting from the collective efforts of the health care industry. I wanted to champion the millions of professionals in the pharmaceutical drug industry who have done so much for our longevity and quality of life, while isolating the 1% bad guys who put patients/consumers at needless risk. I also wanted to research how new regulations through the Drug Quality and Security Act could help prevent bad situations from harming patients/consumers, yet be business-friendly enough not to drive companies out of business and create pharmaceutical drug shortages. It is a delicate balance that our congressional leaders and the Food and Drug Administration (FDA) must achieve with industry leaders to ensure that the cure is not worse than the original symptoms.

For approximately three years, I also had the pleasure of listening to my son speak about return logistics in the pharmaceutical drug industry. It is very obvious that through learning about why things end up in the "supply chain graveyard," supply chain professionals gain key insights on how the forward supply chain process *should* work. When the opportunity came to write this book, I knew my son Karl would be a key contributor in the chapter dealing with return logistics.

The journey is not complete, and in many respects the majority of the work lies ahead for everyone involved. It is my hope that the 99% will prevail, and that I will avoid ever taking penicillin again!

Fred A. Kuglin
Plano, Texas

Acknowledgments

In my opinion, inspiration is the process of being mentally stimulated to do something creative and potentially outside one's comfort zone. Although supply chain management and core knowledge of the pharmaceutical drug industry were within our comfort zone, the world of pharmacy compounding was definitely outside of it. The passing of H.R. 3204 and the reality of the Drug Quality and Security Act gave us—and the industry professionals—a chance to learn and adapt to the new law together.

Fred: As always, a special thanks to my wife of 36 years, Karin, for her patience and encouragement to finish the book, my fifth, and perhaps the most enjoyable to write. A big thank you to the numerous sources within the state boards of pharmacy, most of whom preferred to remain anonymous. One source, Kerstin Arnold with the Texas State Board of Pharmacy, took the time early on to pass along information to me and had the patience to educate me along the way. Special thanks go to Aaron Lopez, Jim Smith, and David Sparks with the Professional Compounding Centers of America (PCCA) and J.D. Willey, Eagle Analytical Services—a PCCA company that opened its doors and provided me an opportunity to observe firsthand the upstream supply chain from source of ingredients to shipments to compounding pharmacies. My thanks to the numerous compounding pharmacy owners and pharmacy retail managers who were willing to talk—albeit anonymously.

In addition, I acknowledge Theresa Weber, PhD, Derma Brands; Michael C. Jarrell, Eli Lilly; Kristin Hunter, McKesson; Ryan Kelly and Rachael Yerges, GENCO; Kristofer Baumgartner and John Swann, FDA (along with numerous anonymous sources within the FDA); Ryon Packer, Authentix; Susan Enzenhofer, TEC-IT; and the managers of my personal pharmacy, Renee and Kathy, for their contributions and permissions for the book.

Recognition goes to Nick Culp and Nick Bush in Representative Fred Upton's office; my numerous anonymous sources in the Drug Enforcement Administration (DEA), Customs and Border Protection (CBP), and various law enforcement agencies; and David J. Ballard, MD, chief quality officer, Baylor Scott & White Health, for their contributions and collective inspiration to complete this book. Recognition goes to Dr. Michael O'Brien and

Heather Bell O'Brien, who worked with me before, during, and after my neck surgery and gave me a renewed respect for all health care professionals. Last but not least, a thank you goes to my son and contributing author, Karl Kuglin, for his contributions to Chapter 7—and the endless dinner conversations regarding pharmaceutical reverse logistics.

Without everyone's contributions, this book would not have been possible.

Karl: Thank you to all my professional colleagues who demonstrated patience while I learned from them. Specifically, I thank Harold Anderson and Robert Fisher in that regard. Both provided me insights into the hard skills in the areas of pharmaceutical drug logistics and operations management. They also gave me a brilliant foundation from which to develop leadership capabilities.

Author

Fred A. Kuglin is president and CEO of Kuglin, Inc., and serves clients at the CXO level in a multitude of industries. He has extensive experience in supply chain management, ePedigree solutions, and start-ups. His expertise is the development of business strategies with the proper implementation activities to produce measurable business performance improvements for clients.

Kuglin has served clients around the world, and has worked for PepsiCo and Ernst & Young LLP as a partner during his career. He has lived in South America as an expat, managing consulting practices in numerous countries. He earned an undergraduate degree from the University of Dayton and an MBA from Indiana University. Kuglin serves on nonprofit boards and leads fund-raisers for worthy causes. He has authored or coauthored numerous books and articles throughout his career. This is the first book he has written with his son, Karl, as a contributing author.

CONTRIBUTING AUTHOR

Karl F. Kuglin is a professional services consultant with Ernst & Young LLP in the EY Life Sciences industry group. He helps pharmaceutical companies adapt and lead change to the industry, including emerging science, new products and services, shifting demographics, evolving regulations (such as the Drug Quality and Security Act), transforming business models, and increased stakeholder expectations.

Kuglin has operational leadership experience with one of the leading return logistics companies in the pharmaceutical industry. This experience includes an in-depth knowledge of the regulations governing pharmaceutical drugs (including controlled substances). He led a team responsible for the receipt, processing, return to manufacturer, and destruction of returned pharmaceutical drugs, and the accuracy of the application for credit allowances to pharmaceutical manufacturers. His contribution to Chapter 7, "When Things Go Bump in the Night: Reverse Logistics," was invaluable. Kuglin is a graduate of Indiana University with a major in business administration.

Introduction: The Good, the Bad, the Ugly, and the Necessary

WHO GIVES IT A SECOND THOUGHT?

In December 2013, our daughter, son-in-law, and 13-month-old grandson came to Texas to visit and spend Christmas with us. They live in Sydney, Australia, and December is summertime for them. Our grandson picked up a bad cold or the flu in his day care, and came to town bearing "gifts" for everyone. It did not take long for all of us to get sick.

A few days after arriving in the States, our daughter was hit particularly hard. Her symptoms were different from the rest of us, though. She woke up in the early morning hours vomiting. At first, we went scrambling to try to figure out what she might have eaten that could have potentially caused food poisoning. She has always had a sensitive digestive system, so we next suspected that the virus from our grandson was manifesting itself differently with her. At no time did we suspect tainted medicine. The pharmaceutical drug industry has performed so well over the past several decades that consumers naturally assume that all pharmaceutical drugs are safe if taken as directed. When was the last time you thought the medicine you were taking was tainted, compromised, or mislabeled?

THE PHARMA INDUSTRY: THE GOOD— POSITIVE IMPACT ON HUMAN LIFE

Throughout the last several decades, the pharmaceutical industry has produced breakthrough pharmaceutical drugs that have contributed to extending the average life span in the United States. One source (see Table I.1) identifies the extension in life expectancy for a person in the

TABLE I.1

Life Expectancy at Birth—United States

	Both Sexes	Male	Female
1930	59.7	58.1	61.6
1970	70.8	67.1	74.7
2010	78.7	76.2	81.1

Source: Modified from http://www.infoplease.com/ipa/A0005148.HTML.

United States from 59.7 years to 78.7 years. This is an astounding increase of 19 years in a short 80-year time span.

A second source, the U.S. Social Security Administration (SSA), identifies a more significant increase. The SSA shows the average life expectancy in the United States increasing from 57 years for both sexes in 1940 (53 male/61 female) to more than 78 years in 2010.[1]

No matter what source is used, the life expectancy in the United States and around the world has increased dramatically over the past several decades. One of the driving forces in the lengthening of life expectancies is the use of vaccines to eradicate or practically eradicate disease. According to the World Health Organization (WHO) and the U.S. Centers for Disease Control and Prevention (CDC), many diseases have been eradicated or practically eradicated. The following is a summary that highlights many of these diseases[2]:

- Diseases eradicated:
  - Smallpox
  - Rinderpest
- Global eradication underway:
  - Polio
  - Dracunculiasis
  - Yaws
- Regional elimination established or underway:
  - Hookworm
  - Malaria
  - Lymphatic filariasis
  - Measles
  - Rubella
  - Onchoceriasis
  - Bovine spongiform encephalopathy (BSE)
- Other eradication efforts:
  - Mumps
  - Cycticercosis

Another source using CDC data shows the following additional diseases recently falling into the practically eradicated category due to vaccines: diphtheria, *Haemophilus influenzae*, hepatitis A, hepatitis B, pertussis, smallpox, tetanus, and varicella.[3]

As consumers, we need to be thankful to the many professionals in the pharmaceutical drug industry who have worked so diligently over the past several decades. From the executives leading the pharmaceutical drug companies to the research professionals developing the vaccines and drugs, our lives have been enriched by their leadership and accomplishments resulting from their tireless efforts.

THE PHARMA INDUSTRY: THE BAD— NEGATIVE IMPACT ON HUMAN LIFE

Unfortunately, in the pharmaceutical drug industry, when bad things happen, people do get hurt. The industry has had its share of issues directly affecting human life. In 1982, seven people died after taking Tylenol® pain-relief medicine capsules that had been poisoned. These poisonings involved Extra-Strength Tylenol capsules, manufactured by McNeil Consumer Healthcare, which had been laced with potassium cyanide. It must be noted that the manufacturing and distribution process for the Extra-Strength Tylenol capsules was intact. The tampering was performed after the capsules were placed on the retail shelves. Johnson & Johnson responded to the crisis with incredible leadership and swift action. The incident led to reforms in the packaging of over-the-counter substances and to federal antitampering laws.[4]

RECALLS—A WAY OF LIFE

Fortunately and unfortunately, recalls in the pharmaceutical drug industry are a way of life. In the last 35 days of 2013 (November 27–December 31, 2013), there were eight recalls by the Food and Drug Administration (FDA) (see Table I.2).[5]

Fast-forward to September and October 2014. There were nine recalls of what the FDA calls Class I, which means there is a reasonable probability

TABLE I.2

FDA Recalls in the Pharmaceutical Drug Industry 11-27-13 to 12-31-13

Date of Recall	Brand Name	Product Description	Reason/Problem	Company
12/30/2013	GE	Multiabsorber original	May have a thin-wall condition that may lead to small holes in the water (drain tube); this may result in a loss of anesthetic gases, ventilation, and oxygenation	Vital Signs Devices
12/23/2013	Hospira	Lidocaine HCI injection	Particulate matter	Hospira
12/23/2013	Burn 7	Dietary supplement	Unapproved new drug	Deseo Rebajar
12/23/2013	Baxter	5% dextrose injection (USP) and 0.9% sodium chloride injection (USP)	Particulate matter	Baxter International
12/18/2013	Abrams Royal Pharmacy	Sterile injectable medications	Potential for microbial contamination	Abrams Royal Pharmacy
12/13/2013	Soliris	Soliris (eculizumab) 300 mg/30 ml concentrated solution for intravenous infusion only	Found to contain visible particles	Alexion Pharmaceuticals
11/27/2013	FreeStyle®, FreeStyleLite®	Blood glucose test strips	May produce erroneously low blood glucose results	Abbott
11/27/2013	Baxter	Nitroglycerin in 5% dextrose injection	Particulates	Baxter International

Source: Modified from http://www.fda.gov/Drugs/drugsafety/DrugRecalls/default.htm.
Note: USP, U.S. Pharmacopeia.

TABLE I.3

FDA Recalls in the Pharmaceutical Drug Industry 9-6-14 to 10-20-14

Date of Recall	Brand Name	Product Description	Reason/Problem	Company
10/20/2014	Assured Brand	Naproxen sodium tablets	Voluntary recall due to packaging mix-up	Contract Packaging Resources
10/16/2014	Hospira	One lot of 1% lidocaine HCl injection (USP), 10 mg/ml, 30 ml single dose	Voluntary recall due to particulate matter	Hospira
10/14/2014	Hospira	Selected lots of LifeCare products	Voluntary recall due to potential for leakage	Hospira
10/9/2014	Oregon Compounding Centers	Unexpired sterile products in Oregon and Washington	Voluntary recall due to lack of sterility assurance	Oregon Compounding Centers
10/7/2014	Hospira	One lot of vancomycin hydrochloride for injection (USP)	Voluntary recall due to uncontrolled storage during transit	Hospira
10/3/2014	Sagent	Three lots of ketorolac tromethamine injection (USP), 30 mg/MI	Nationwide voluntary recall due to labeling the product with the incorrect expiration date	Sagent Pharmaceuticals
9/16/2014	Baxter	One lot of potassium chloride injection	Voluntary recall due to shipping carton mislabeling	Baxter
9/11/2014	Hospira	One lot of heparin sodium, 1,000 USP heparin units/500 ml (2 USP heparin units)	Voluntary nationwide recall due to particulate matter	Hospira
9/6/2014	Pharmacy Creations	Four product lots	Voluntary recall in Florida, New Jersey, New York, and Puerto Rico due to potential nonsterility	Pharmacy Creations

Source: Modified from http://www.fda.gov/Drugs/drugsafety/DrugRecalls/default.htm.
Note: USP, U.S. Pharmacopeia.

that the use of or exposure to the identified products will cause either adverse health consequences or death (Table I.3).[6]

To be fair, many of the FDA recalls are initiated by the pharmaceutical drug companies as voluntary recalls through their own internal quality control activities. Having said this, if I was a heart patient and received nitroglycerin from Baxter, or if I had diabetes and used the blood glucose test strips from Abbott, I would be very nervous.

In addition, during the past decade there has been rampant misuse of pharmaceutical drugs, causing eye-popping numbers of fatalities. In October 2013, there were more deaths from drug overdoses than auto accidents in 29 states and the District of Columbia! At the top of the list of abused drugs are prescription painkillers, including, but not limited, to OxyContin, Percocet®, and Vicodin®.[7] One Drug Enforcement Administration (DEA) official privately told me that the move to legalize the recreational use of marijuana in several states (Colorado, Washington, Oregon, and Alaska) and the growth of homemade meth labs has shifted the focus of organized crime groups away from traditional drugs such as marijuana and meth to controlled substance pharmaceutical drugs—specifically, prescription painkillers. Unfortunately, pharmaceutical drugs intended to enhance human life can be and are abused, destroying human life in the process.

There are silver linings to these issues. The Tylenol tragedy resulted in the pharmaceutical drug industry transitioning to solid caplets and away from easy-to-tamper capsules. The FDA introduced new product-tampering regulations, including tamper-evident safety seals, which we see on food items as well as pharma drugs. Most companies that go through product recalls use them to do root cause analyses on the issues and make the necessary changes for continuous improvements in their policies, procedures, and processes. For the companies that produce the pharmaceutical drugs that are most abused, such as prescription painkillers, stringent packaging and stronger chain-of-custody procedures have been instituted to help reduce the unauthorized availability of these drugs.

THE PHARMA INDUSTRY: THE UGLY—HUMAN LIFE LOST

The global pharmaceutical drug industry is huge. No matter what sources you choose, the numbers are staggering. Current estimates are that the industry (inclusive of wholesalers, distributors, pharmacies, etc.) has approximately $1 trillion in revenue, and is expected to exceed $2 trillion by 2018. The pharmaceutical manufacturing companies themselves are expected to increase revenues to $1.2 trillion in 2018. Industry experts estimate the global pharmaceutical industry employs between 1.5 million and 2.0 million people.[8]

As in any industry, the actions of a few at times overshadow the efforts of the industry overall. In addition, employees are people, complete with all the strengths and weaknesses associated with being human. Mistakes are made—sometimes by accident, sometimes by negligence, and sometimes by willful intent. If 99% of the pharmaceutical drug employees work within the rules and focus on balancing patient safety with making a profit, society is still left with the 1%, or approximately 20,000 employees, potentially participating in proscribed behavior.

In October 2012, an unthinkable, ugly incident happened. An outbreak of fungal meningitis was reported by the CDC. The CDC traced the outbreak to fungal contamination in three lots of medicine used for epidural steroid injections. The three lots were produced by the New England Compounding Center (NECC) in Framingham, Massachusetts. The CDC reported that the tainted medicine was administered to approximately 14,000 patients, with 751 contracting meningitis and 64 dying. Federal inspectors found dirty mats, black specks floating around in vials, and other signs of contamination at the Framingham operation.[9]

The state of Massachusetts conducted surprise visits to other compounding facilities in October 2012, shutting down two more compounding pharmacies. In additional surprise visits in December 2012, problems were found in three more pharmacies.[10] Among industry experts and politicians alike, the consensus was that the oversight for compounding pharmacies was severely lacking.

Consensus stopped with the premise that more oversight is needed of these operations. There was (and still is) a lot of finger pointing as to who is the responsible party for the oversight activities. The FDA points to the Massachusetts State Board of Pharmacy and other agencies, the Massachusetts state agencies point to the FDA, and they both point to the compounding companies. The issue is not an easy one to address. Compounding is the custom making or mixing of medicines for individuals who need specialty drugs not readily available in the marketplace. Two medicines can be made in two states, shipped to a third state for mixing, with the final product being distributed in multiple states. The final manufacturing point is in one state (as was the case with the NECC in Massachusetts), while the distribution can take place in multiple states (the NECC shipped the tainted medicine to 20 states).[10] Who is in charge of enforcement? When confusion occurs, enforcement falls back on the companies and their owners/employees. We all hope for the 99% factor to take place. It is ugly when the 1% factor occurs.

THE PHARMA INDUSTRY: THE NECESSARY— THE DRUG QUALITY AND SECURITY ACT (H.R. 3204)

In a rare show of bipartisan support, Congress passed the Drug Quality and Security Act (H.R. 3204) in response to the NECC fungal meningitis outbreak. President Obama signed this act into law on November 27, 2013. The Drug Quality and Security Act clarifies the authority of the FDA to regulate specialty compounded drugs, creates a new voluntary program for the FDA to regulate entities that participate in batch compounding that elect to register with the FDA, and establishes authority for the FDA to develop a national track-and-trace system to secure the pharmaceutical supply chain and minimize the opportunity for contamination, adulteration, diversion, or counterfeiting.[11]

Sometimes pharmaceutical drug laws are created to fix or cure a breakdown in current laws that govern processes, policies, and procedures in the pharmaceutical drug supply chain. In the case of the Drug Quality and Security Act, the jury is still out on the "cure." Congress has been known to pass laws that intend to fix problems but make matters more bureaucratic and worse in the long run. The problem with compounding mistakes is that they can be ugly, in this case resulting in 64 deaths and 751 infections. Something needed to be done.

The good news is that we did determine why my daughter had different symptoms than the rest of the family. As it turned out, she was pregnant with our second grandchild!

THE BOOK CHAPTERS

Chapter 1 starts with the FDA Modernization Act of 1997. It proceeds through the *Thompson versus Western States* litigation on the part of the law that prevented compound manufacturers from marketing and advertising. Two appeals courts rendered two different decisions on the constitutionality of the clause, which caused chaos in the industry until it was addressed by H.R. 3204. This chapter reviews how H.R. 3204 and laws in general are made in the U.S. Congress and signed by the president. It proceeds through a level set of definitions of compounding that will be beneficial as we proceed through the book. It also showcases several states and how they are doing their part to complement and extend H.R. 3204 in their areas of responsibility.

In Chapter 2, we define pharmacy compounding at a deeper level and show examples of nonsterile compounding solutions and compounded medicines that are sterile for office use. We introduced the Drug Quality and Security Act and Title I: Compounding Quality Act, and discuss the Food and Drug Modernization Act of 1997 as a prelude to the Drug Quality and Security Act. We revisit Section 503A, showing why its exemptions are so important by identifying the extensive process of FDA trials for new drugs. We then look at Section 503B and outsourcing facility registration and reporting. We discuss some issues to be resolved and have an in-depth look at governance and leadership. We also discuss how breakdowns occurred in these areas with the NECC, potentially contributing to additional and unnecessary infections and loss of life.

Chapter 3 takes a look at the safety of the compounding supply chain under the spirit of the Drug Quality and Security Act. We review three main parts to this supply chain: from doctor prescription/patient demand to ingredients, ingredients to compounding pharmacies, and compounding pharmacies to patients in need of the compounded medicines. We review the Pharmacy Compounding Centers of America (PCCA) in depth, from patient prescription to the delivery of the needed ingredients to a compounding pharmacy to fill the prescription. We also review compounding pharmacies to patients, and at a very high level discuss clean rooms for sterile compounding of drugs. In addition, we look at current good manufacturing practices in some depth, and propose a new service for the compounding pharmacies. We briefly discuss good laboratory practices and good clinical practices. At the end of the chapter we review Eagle Analytical Services and their support of compounding pharmacies, such as testing samples and formulas and providing feedback techniques to pharmacists at compounding pharmacies.

We start Chapter 4 by identifying that the Title II: Drug Supply Chain Security Act has three objectives: (1) enable verification of the legitimacy of the drug product identifier down to the package level, (2) enhance detection and notification of illegitimate products in the drug supply chain, and (3) facilitate more efficient recalls of drug products. We review the seven key provisions of Title II, and compare the past ePedigree initiative with Title II. We also introduce three companies (Authentix, Tracelink, and One Network) that have capabilities to meet or exceed FDA requirements in Title II regarding authentication, tracking, and tracing pharmaceutical drugs.

In Chapter 5 we discuss how the pharmaceutical drug wholesale distributor industry is close to an oligopoly, with the dominant market share (85%) controlled by the "big three": McKesson, AmerisourceBergen, and Cardinal Health. We review the big three, including their rich histories, and in a couple of cases trace their origins to the 1800s. This industry has large revenues and asset bases but razor-thin operating margins. The FDA is walking a fine line to implement needed reforms, but not to the extent of pushing the wholesale distributors out of business.

The Title II: Drug Supply Chain Security Act is intended to secure the supply chain through mandating transaction information, transaction history, and a transaction statement for pharmaceutical drugs as they change ownership from manufacturer to the patient or consumer. We cover these new regulations in depth. The wholesale distributors participating in repackaging programs for pharmacies and hospitals will have to comply with the new regulations. These regulations are placing repackagers and pharmaceutical drug manufacturers in the same group, and need to affix unique product identifiers to the packaging. This will add cost and complexity to their repackaging operations.

In Chapter 6, we review how the Title II: Drug Supply Chain Security Act will help improve the security of the pharmacy prescription order-fill process. We discuss how only 3% of the online or Internet pharmacies are legitimate, while 97% are not. We also review the health and financial risks associated with using illegal online Internet pharmacies to purchase drugs. In addition, we discuss pill mills in some depth, how Florida is combating these pill mills, and the responsibility of local pharmacists (the consumer/patient touchpoint) to monitor abnormal usage regarding the ordering and dispensing of selected pharmaceutical drugs.

In Chapter 7 we discuss logistics. Reverse logistics is defined as the supply chain in reverse. Pharmaceutical drug returns occur because of excess supply or saleable returns, unsaleable returns, and recalled drugs. Reverse distributors primarily handle pharmaceutical drug returns. As with wholesale distributors, reverse distributors have their own "big three." The big three reverse distributors are GENCO, Inmar, and Stericycle. They have rich histories and offer a wide variety of returns services. The Drug Quality and Security Act largely ignores returns. However, we review how Title II of the Drug Quality and Security Act, through its mandated product identifiers and product tracking, provides a wonderful opportunity for pharmaceutical drug companies to determine the why behind returns. We show the connection between the why behind the returns and how to lower the cost of returns through adjustments in the forward supply chain.

Chapter 8 covers the "lettered" government agencies. There are several agencies that are responsible for various aspects of the pharmaceutical drug supply chain. We review the two primary federal agencies and three primary state agencies. The FDA is responsible for protecting the public health by assuring the safety, efficacy, and security of human drugs (among other responsibilities). We review the history of the FDA and how we got to the Drug Quality and Security Act. The DEA enforces the controlled substances laws and regulations of the United States. We review the history of the DEA and its intersection with the FDA on the Drug Quality and Security Act. We also review the three state agencies: the state boards of pharmacy that regulate pharmacists; the state departments of public safety that fill in the gaps at the local level and enforce all federal and state laws regarding the manufacture, transport, warehousing, delivery, and dispensing of pharmaceutical drugs; and the state medical boards that regulate the doctors writing the prescriptions.

In Chapter 9, we start by defining public policy, and then proceed to trace major pharmaceutical drug legislation to major incidents involving illnesses and deaths. We proceed to take a look at innovation, and specifically review a compounding drug example. We then look at drug shortages, and how unanswered questions with the Drug Quality and Security Act can contribute to shortages of compounded drugs through competent compounders exiting the business. We briefly revisit the FDA trials process, and how accelerating the process can help prevent drug shortages. We include the Ebola crisis as an example, and how the Ebola crisis intersects with the FDA trial process and public policy. We proceed to look at the Drug Quality and Security Act, and how it impacts pharmaceutical drug companies and trucking companies. We conclude the chapter with a brief look at the role nurses play with drug quality and drug security.

Chapter 10 details the drug quality and security "hall of fame." Throughout history, there have been numerous people who have significantly contributed to drug quality and drug security. From leaders of countries and legislators to research specialists, from pharmacists to emergency room nurses, and from wholesale distributor repackaging specialists to receiving supervisors in returns and logistics providers, people have made a difference. In this chapter, we showcase a few individuals who distinguished themselves and truly made a difference. These people are David Sparks, founder of PCCA; the four Lillys (Colonel Eli the founder, Josiah Sr., Eli, and Josiah Jr.) of Eli Lilly and Company; John McKesson, founder, and Neil E. Harmon and Alan Seelenfreund, CEOs, McKesson and Company; Herb Sheer, CEO of GENCO and grandson of GENCO's founder, Dr. Harvey W. Wiley, sponsor of the Pure Foods and Drugs Act of 1906; Representative Fred Upton, sponsor of the Drug Quality and Security Act of 2013; and Dr. David J. Ballard, chief quality officer, Baylor Scott & White Health and president of STEEEP Global Institute, Baylor Health Care System.

ENDNOTES

1. Life Expectancy for Social Security, Social Security, http://www.ssa.gov/history/lifeexpect.html.
2. Health Topics, World Health Organization, http://www.who.int/topics/en/; Diseases and Conditions, Centers for Disease Control and Prevention, http://www.cdc.gov/DiseasesConditions/.
3. Tara Culp-Ressler, Vaccines Have Almost Totally Eliminated These Thirteen Infectious Diseases in the U.S., Think Progress, 2013, http://thinkprogress.org/health/2013/02/22/1622871/vaccines-impact-infographic.
4. Tamara Kaplan, The Tylenol Crisis: How Effective Public Relations Saved Johnson & Johnson, Pennsylvania State University, 1996.
5. Drug Recalls, U.S. Food and Drug Administration, http://www.fda.gov/Drugs/drugsafety/DrugRecalls/default.htm.
6. Ibid.
7. Reid Wilson, Drug Overdoses Kill More People than Auto Accidents in 29 States, *The Washington Post*, 2013, http://www.washingtonpost.com/blogs/govbeat/wp/2013/10/08/drug-overdoses-kill-more-people-than-auto-accidents-in-29-states.
8. Research and Markets: Global Market for Dendrimers 2010–2015, Yahoo! Finance, http://finance.yahoo.com/news/research-markets-global-pharmaceutical-industry-153100399.html.
9. Todd Wallack, $100 Million Agreement Close in Meningitis Outbreak Case, *The Boston Globe*, 2013, http://www.bostonglobe.com/metro/2013/12/23/meningitis/E97yWKhnC2LyI HRek4KjKJ/story.html.
10. Ibid.
11. Statement by the Press Secretary on H.R. 1848, H.R. 3204, S. 252, The White House, http://www.whitehouse.gov/the-press-office/2013/11/27/statement-press-secretary-hr-1848-hr-3204-s-252.

1

H.R. 3204: The Journey and Expected Destination

HOW DID WE GET TO NOVEMBER 27, 2013?

The date November 27, 2013, has a dual meaning for me. Not only did President Obama sign H.R. 3204 into law, but on this date, I had neck surgery to straighten my neck and fuse my C6 and C7 vertebrae. My surgery was necessary (the pain was excruciating with a completely disintegrated disc and the shifting of two vertebrae squeezing two different nerve roots). For me, the surgery was a success. Sometimes surgery on the neck and spine creates more pain, with the "cure" being worse than the problem.

My personal journey to November 27, 2013, and my neck surgery started at birth. My primary care physician said genetically I had a predisposition for neck problems. (I am sure I did things in life that did not help matters regarding my neck condition.) As far as the Drug Quality and Security Act, it was not the first law to try to address regulations on pharmaceutical drugs. In Chapter 8, we take an in-depth look at the Food and Drug Administration (FDA) and the history of pharmaceutical drug regulations. For now, let's focus on the compounding of drugs and the recent attempts to regulate them. The Drug Quality and Security Act amended the FDA Modernization Act of 1997. Let's take a look at the FDA Modernization Act of 1997.

THE FDA MODERNIZATION ACT OF 1997

According to the FDA, the FDA Modernization Act of 1997 (FDAMA) is a major legislation focused on reforming the regulation of food, medical products, and cosmetics. The following are the most important provisions of the act:

- Prescription drug user fees
- FDA initiatives and programs
- Information on off-label use and drug economics
- Pharmacy compounding
- Risk-based regulation of medical devices
- Food safety and labeling
- Standards for medical products[1]

Under the pharmacy compounding provision, the FDA provides this summary:

> The act creates a special exemption to ensure continued availability of compounded drug products prepared by pharmacists to provide patients with individualized therapies not available commercially. The law, however, seeks to prevent manufacturing under the guise of compounding by establishing parameters within which the practice is appropriate and lawful.[2]

These are well-written intentions of the FDAMA in 1997, but still people throughout the pharmaceutical supply chain wanted to know what happened. This includes legislative/elected officials and patients like you and me. To pursue the answer to this question, I took a deeper dive into the FDAMA.

Section 127 of FDAMA added Section 503A to the FFDCA (remember, the FDAMA amended the FFDCA). Section 503A exempted compounded drugs from new drug laws as long as the compounded drug met several conditions/restrictions. Included in the new drug laws were the myriad and lengthy new drug requirements (FDA trials, etc.), as well as the labeling requirements. Another key condition was that the compounded drug had to be produced using current good manufacturing practices (cGMP). We will review cGMP in more depth in Chapter 2.

One big issue with FDAMA, Sections 127 and 503A, was that drug providers were prohibited from soliciting and advertising particular compounded drugs. One legislative aide who is still working for a congressman (and wishes to remain anonymous) gave me some insight on the logic behind this provision. He said,

> We thought if we would exempt compounded drugs from the new drug requirements and labeling, as long as they were manufactured under cGMPs and met the other provisions of FDAMA, we could control the "process of production." We believed that by prohibiting the solicitation and advertising of the compounded drugs to office users, we could limit their activities as a manufacturer and force the compounders to work on a "patient pull" system. This way everything the compounding pharmacies produced would directly fill individual patient prescriptions.

In theory and in a simple world, this logic made sense. However, what happened next could be categorized as either unintended consequences or mass confusion (or both).

THOMPSON VERSUS WESTERN STATES MEDICAL CENTER

A group of licensed pharmacies that specialize in compounding drugs (Western States Medical Center, now Kronos Compounding Pharmacy) filed suit to enjoin enforcement of the advertising and solicitation provisions in 503A, arguing that they violate the First Amendment's free speech guarantee. The district court agreed, and held that the provisions constituted unconstitutional restrictions on commercial speech. The court of appeals concluded that the government had not demonstrated that the restrictions would directly advance its interests or that alternatives less restrictive of speech were unavailable.

The Supreme Court took the case and specifically addressed the following question: *Do the prohibitions in the Food and Drug Administration Modernization Act of 1997 with regard to soliciting prescriptions for and advertising compounded drugs violate the First Amendment?*

On April 29, 2002, in a 5–4 opinion delivered by Justice Sandra Day O'Connor, the court held that the FDAMA's provisions in 503A amounted to unconstitutional restrictions on commercial speech. Among other findings, the court reasoned that although the speech restrictions allegedly served governmental interests in permitting drug compounding while guaranteeing that compounding was not conducted on such a scale as to undermine the drug approval process, it had not been demonstrated that the speech restrictions were not more extensive than necessary to serve such interests.[3]

ARE WE MAKING PROGRESS?

Unfortunately, the Supreme Court did not address whether the remaining provisions in 503A remained "good law." After five years, the compounding pharmacy industry was now in a total state of confusion. What was the current status of compounding drugs, and what was expected from the compounding pharmacies in terms of compliance? What regulatory body was responsible for monitoring compounding pharmacies? Were the advertising and solicitation provisions "severable" from 503A, or was the entire 503A section struck down?

SO WHERE ARE WE?

On July 30, 2002, the FDA came out with a draft of its FDA Compliance Policy Guidelines and said in essence it was not in a hurry to address the issue of 503A. It said, "Moreover, the practice of pharmacy, including compounding, is heavily regulated by the State Boards of Pharmacy." Ultimately, the FDA would decide it had a case for enforcement.[4]

A group of pharmacies pushed back against the FDA's authority for oversight. On July 18, 2008, the Fifth Circuit Court in *Medical Center Pharmacy v. Mukasey* found that the other provisions in 503A were lawful and still in effect. The FDA would go on to say that it could exercise discretion in taking action against a compounding pharmacy that violated the 503A provisions.[5]

So in 2001 we have the Ninth Circuit Court in *Western States v. Shalala* determining that 503A was struck down in its entirety, leading up to the Supreme Court decision in 2002.[6] We have the Fifth Circuit Court determining that the free speech provision was severable and the remaining 503A section was in force. What we ended up with was a situation of nonuniform enforcement by the FDA—and total confusion.

What was the law of the land, and what agency was in charge of monitoring compounding pharmacies? The reality was that no one seemed to know. According to my legislative aide source, most people thought the entire compounding section of the FDAMA had been struck down and was now invalid.

BLUE STATE, PURPLE STATE, RED STATE— NOW IT MAKES SENSE

When I first started my research for this book, I called the state boards of pharmacy in two big blue states, a good size purple state, and two big red states. The representative of one of the blue state boards of pharmacy said in so many words that they wait until the FDA tells them the rules, and then they follow them. The representative of the purple state board of pharmacy said they were in a push-pull between following the FDA and initiating legislation to do their own oversight. I thought their actions were politically in line with federal government versus state government rights. However, there was a legal reason for the differences. The red states are in the Fifth Circuit, while the blue states are in the Ninth Circuit, with the purple state falling under the "all other" states.

It took the unfortunate incident with the New England Compounding Center (NECC) and the loss of life to trigger legislative action to address the confusion. In many ways, the legislative action was "confusion to solve confusion."

HOW H.R. 3204 BECAME LAW

H.R. 3204 is otherwise known as the Drug Quality and Security Act.[7] In terms of the U.S. Congress, this law was passed swiftly and with bipartisan support. Some people who lobby the U.S. Congress for a living sometimes equate the process to make a law with the process to make sausage. It is not pretty, but eventually the outcome is positive for our nation.

All laws have to begin with ideas. The thought of doing nothing after 751 people contracted meningitis and 64 people lost their lives after being administered with tainted medicine was not even considered by

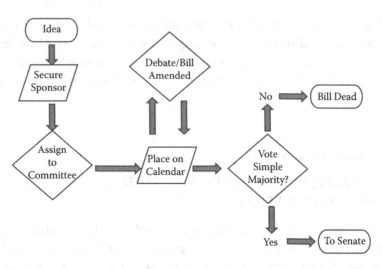

FIGURE 1.1

How laws are made—simplified House of Representatives process. (Adapted by Fred Kuglin from http://www.house.gov/content/learn/legislative_process.)

the House of Representatives. The idea to protect our pharmaceutical drug supply originated with several representatives. The next step was to get a sponsor for the bill. Representative Fred Upton (R-Michigan Sixth District) sponsored the bill, introducing it to the House of Representatives on September 27, 2013. The Drug Quality and Security Act bill was immediately referred to the U.S. House Energy and Commerce Committee. The bill was not debated or amended. The House voted on September 28, 2013, to pass the bill in a voice vote.[8]

Fred is the U.S. House Energy and Commerce Committee chairman. He holds a powerful position in the House, lending credence and importance to the bill by being its sponsor. In addition, there were 3 deaths in Representative Upton's district, while there were 264 infections and 22 deaths in the state of Michigan associated with the New England Compounding Center meningitis outbreak (Figure 1.1).[9]

The H.R. 3204 bill was received in the Senate on September 30, 2013. It was placed on the legislative calendar, and the Senate began debate on the bill on November 12, 2013. Senator David Vitter (R-LA) filibustered the bill to try to get the Senate to amend H.R. 3204 and pass the Show Your Exemption Act. That bill would mandate all House of Representatives and Senators to disclose the members of their staffs they elected to exempt from enrolling in insurance through an Obamacare exchange. Cloture was

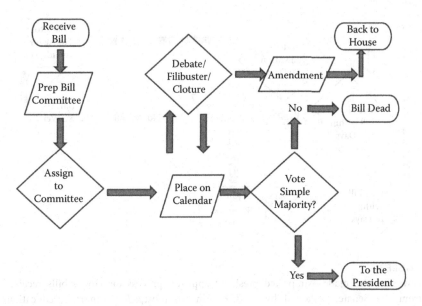

FIGURE 1.2
How laws are made—simplified Senate process for House bills. (Adapted by Fred Kuglin from https://votesmart.org/education/how-a-bill-becomes-law.)

invoked, and the Senate voted 97–1 to begin working on the bill with no amendments. Senator Vitter was the only no vote.[10]

On November 18, H.R. 3204 was passed in the Senate by voice vote. The bill immediately was sent to President Obama for his signature (Figure 1.2).[11]

As I mentioned in the introduction, President Obama signed H.R. 3204 into law on November 27, 2013. H.R. 3204 officially became the Drug Quality and Security Act. The president completed the cycle of a bill being introduced into the House of Representatives by the signing of the bill into law. The sausage was made!

As President Obama was signing H.R. 3204 into law, I was in the recovery room with my wife. In recovery, I had no idea what drugs were given to me or if they were compounded to accommodate my surgery. In addition, I had so many presurgery tests that I had no clue if I had used a compounded drug for any of them (i.e., CT scan with a myelogram). As a patient, I had faith that everyone—from my surgeon to my primary care physician, from the nurses to the supporting staff at the hospital, from the numerous specialists to the janitorial staff that clean the operating and recovery rooms, and from the pharmaceutical companies to all of their supply chain partners—was doing their job and my surgery would be a success.

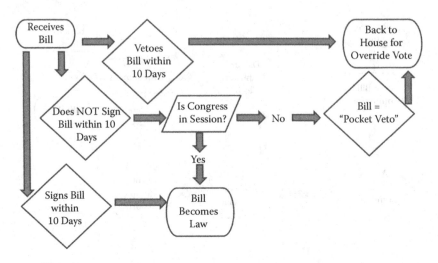

FIGURE 1.3

How laws are made—simplified president approval process for House bills received from the Senate. (Adapted by Fred Kuglin from https://votesmart.org/education/how-a-bill-becomes-law.)

I was given—and took a lot of—pharmaceutical drugs from the time of my admittance until my discharge from the hospital. The only issue was a push-pull between my primary care physician and the head nurse. My primary care physician was stressing the need for me to use the morphine pump for my pain, while the head nurse was stressing the need for me to get up (painful with a rebuilt neck) and walk to the bathroom on my own. I told both of them that when I used the morphine pump, the floor started moving and there was no way I was in any condition to navigate going to the bathroom with a moving floor.

We are fortunate that the medical profession and pharmaceutical drug industry have come so far that patients rely on them as safe. I believe this is what the intended outcome of H.R. 3204 was when it was introduced by Representative Fred Upton—the reinforcement of the safety of compounded drugs (Figure 1.3).

ONCE AGAIN, WHAT JUST HAPPENED—AND HOW DID WE GET TO THE DRUG QUALITY AND SECURITY ACT?

In January 2014, I placed a call to the legislative office of one of the major sponsors of the bill. One of the legislative aides answered the phone. I asked,

"What just happened with H.R. 3204, or the Drug Quality and Security Act?" The answer I received was, "We just fixed everything that was wrong legislatively with drug compounding and track and trace." I asked, "Can you elaborate on this?" In fact, I tried three times, and finally I received an honest, non-campaign–type answer: "We set in motion the ability of the FDA and state regulatory boards to share oversight responsibilities of drug compounding and clear up the confusion of 503A. In addition, we set in motion the ability of the FDA to define the requirements for track and trace and fix what we did wrong with ePedigree six to seven years ago."

Uh-oh. Another law was passed where the actual requirements of the law for the supply chain participants to be in compliance were "to be determined" (TBD). And track and trace? Are we "back to the future" with a modified ePedigree law? So now we are embracing all supply chain participants beyond compounding pharmacies in the new law.

QUICK LEVEL SET OF DEFINITIONS

Pharmaceutical compounding is the creation of a particular pharmaceutical drug product or medicine to fit the unique need of a patient. When a given pharmaceutical drug product is made or modified to have characteristics that are specifically prescribed for an individual patient, it is known as *traditional compounding*. When pharmaceutical compounding is done on bulk production of a given formulation rather than patient-specific production, it is known as nontraditional compounding or *compound manufacturing*. When pharmaceutical compounding is done for a specific hospital, medical facility, or a medical practice (such as a scoliosis institute) that tightly assembles patient prescriptions, it is known as *compounding for office use* or *compounding outsourcing*.[12]

One expert in this area (whose opinion I highly value) believes that the last two, compound manufacturing and compounding for office use or compounding outsourcing, are basically the same. One compounding pharmacy owner in Texas disagrees. He sells compounded medicines on a daily basis to about a dozen large physician-owned practices. These physician-owned practices place their orders with this compounding pharmacy for specific, next-day patients and their prescriptions. He said, "We have a new law, but once again, the question of what is traditional compounding versus what is compound manufacturing still persists. All that work in Washington, D.C., and everything is still clear as mud!" For the sake of the book, we will draw a dotted line between the two definitions.

THE STATES—TAG, YOU'RE IT!

The states and the state boards of pharmacy have always regulated pharmacists. As we mentioned, there was a gray area between the FDA and the state boards of pharmacy on who had oversight responsibility for compounding pharmacies. After the Drug Quality and Security Act was signed into law, a number of states enacted legislation to come into compliance with the Drug Quality and Security Act and try to "fill the gaps." Let's review a few of the key states and their legislative responses to this new law.

Massachusetts: Their Response

To the credit of the state of Massachusetts, they became proactive in their efforts to address a gray area between the FDA and the Massachusetts State Board of Pharmacy regarding oversight of compounding pharmacies. On July 10, 2014, Governor Deval Patrick signed into law the Massachusetts Compounding Pharmacy Oversight Bill. This new law includes (among other items) new licensing and labeling requirements, steps up fines for violations of state rules, and requires the board's inspectors to be trained in sterile and nonsterile compounding practices. "I think this puts us ahead of other states," Patrick said after a statehouse bill-signing ceremony. "The gray area that I and so many other people talked about is an area of considerable ambiguity about where state authority leaves off and federal authority begins."[13]

Personally, I think he is correct on multiple counts. The FDA now regulates compound manufacturers. The state boards of pharmacy regulate traditional compounding. Who regulates the compounding pharmacies that compound medicines for office use? In addition, as we will see in Chapter 2, there is a big difference between sterile and nonsterile compounding of medicines.

This bill also created four new specialty licenses: a retail sterile compounding specialty license, a retail complex nonsterile compounding specialty license, an institutional pharmacy specialty license, which applies to hospitals, and an out-of-state pharmacy license for out-of-state pharmacies doing business in Massachusetts. The latter license is extremely important for states, since so many compounding pharmacies producing medicines for office use ship medicines across state lines to their customers.[14]

Michigan: Representative Fred Upton's State

Michigan was perhaps the hardest hit state from the NECC fungal meningitis outbreak. As we mentioned earlier, of the 751 cases of fungal meningitis infections and 64 deaths, Michigan accounted for 264 infections and 22 deaths. State Senator Joe Hune, R-Hamburg, sponsored Senate Bills 704 and 904 to address and reform state licensing methods when a public health risk is present. These bills passed the Michigan State Senate and were signed into law by Governor Rick Snyder on July 2, 2014. Senate Bill 904 became Public Act 279, and Senate Bill 704 became Public Act 280.[15]

The state of Michigan took a different route in regulating compounding pharmacies. They now require that accurate records of compounding pharmacy procedures be maintained. They also require a state inspection of every compounding pharmacy in Michigan every two years, and a pharmacist-in-charge be designated to make sure the compounding pharmacy is compliant with state regulations. In addition, criminal penalties were added for violations that result in patient injury (maximum 4-year sentence) or death (maximum 15-year sentence).[16]

I totally understand the state inspection or audit, and will cover a recommendation on this in Chapter 3. The record keeping of compounding pharmacy procedures, inclusive of calculations and formulas to fill prescriptions of office use orders, is something that we all assume is done by compounding pharmacies. At least it is done now in Michigan.

California

California was not affected by the NECC fungal meningitis outbreak. However, California is not a state to miss out on a regulation party. The state is always quick to apply regulations in multiple industries. One of my friends who lives in Southern California told me if the lawmakers in Sacramento could figure out a way to regulate regulators and fund it, they would do so in a heartbeat!

On October 4, 2013 (before H.R. 3204 passed the U.S. Senate and was signed into law by President Obama), the governor of California signed into law Senate Bill 294. This bill changed the California pharmacy law, and requires the licensing of all pharmacies, resident and nonresident, that compound sterile, injectable drug products and others for dispensing in the state of California. It also provides a path for physical inspections of nonresident pharmacies that compound sterile, injectable drug products and others and ship these products into California for dispensing. The pharmacies that produce the sterile compound medicines are also required to prepare a written master formula record for each product.[17]

Florida

The state of Florida has come a long way in the past 10–15 years in terms of pharmaceutical drug regulations. When the Drug Quality and Security Act was signed into law, the Florida Board of Pharmacy rules allowed pharmacies to engage in office use compounding. Specifically, these rules allowed physicians to use compounded medicines to treat patients in their offices. They did not allow physicians to dispense compounded medicines to their patients. The Florida Board of Pharmacy made the decision after the Drug Quality and Security Act on May 1, 2014, to rule that all sterile pharmaceutical drugs produced by licensed compounding pharmacies must be for specific patients. All other compounded medicines, including for office use, must be done by a registered outsourcing facility. When I inquired by phone with the Florida Board of Pharmacy, I was told they made this strict definition to ensure that Florida pharmacies holding a sterile compounding permit did not make any mistakes and unknowingly violate the new federal law.[18]

Needless to say, I am impressed. Florida drew a hard line where the line was blurred and subject to interpretation. Florida pharmacies can now only compound sterile pharmaceutical drug products for human use directly for patients with prescriptions. All office use compound sterile pharmaceutical drug products must be produced by licensed outsourcing facilities. The Florida Board of Pharmacy now mandates that hospitals and medical practices can only procure their sterile compounded medicines from licensed outsourcing facilities.

Personally, I still believe that the smaller compounding pharmacies that produce sterile pharmaceutical drug products for physicians *on a daily basis* are producing for specific patients. However, Florida took a practical approach to implement the new law and minimize the gray area. I hope the smaller compounding pharmacies do not elect to go out of business, rather than choose to be licensed outsourcing facilities. The additional regulations are ominous, and if the smaller compounding pharmacies exit the business, problems with supply of compounded medicines could occur for patients in need.

Colorado

The Colorado State Board of Pharmacy recently enacted SB14-095: Pharmacies Compounding Drugs for Hospitals. Under the old law, a prescription drug outlet could only distribute compounded drugs for office use to physicians/practitioners who are authorized to prescribe drugs. The SB14-095 law allows prescription drug outlets to distribute compounded drugs to hospitals within the state of Colorado.[19] There are limitations with this new law. In Colorado, the Department of Regulatory Agencies (DORA) is responsible for promulgating rules that limit the amount of drugs a prescription drug outlet can compound to a hospital. The limit under SB14-095 is to be no more than 10% of the total number of dosage units the prescription drug outlet dispenses on an annual basis.[20] In my opinion, I have mixed feelings on the dosage limit, but overall I believe this is a very good bill. Hospitals are looking to outsource more of their compounding medicines for inpatients to pharmacies specializing in compounding, and this increases the availability of options and supply for them.

Texas

The Texas State Board of Pharmacy (TSBP) has been active in doing its best to comply with the Drug Quality and Security Act. It regulates pharmacies compounding drugs under its TSBP Rule 291.133: Pharmacies Compounding Sterile Preparations. It extended its regulations through the enactment of TSBP Rule 291.76(d)(1)(L), which became effective August 31, 2014. Under this new rule, a pharmacy shall not compound sterile preparations unless the pharmacy has applied for and obtained a Class C-S license. Under this new license, pharmacies must register annually or biennially following the procedures specified in TSBP Rule 291.133, and must be inspected by TSBP prior to being issued a Class C-S license or renewing its license.[21]

Also, effective September 1, 2015, all personnel engaged in sterile compounding in any manner will need to have completed a single course, a minimum of 20 to 40 hours of instruction, from an accredited Council for Pharmacy Education approved provider, and completed a structured on-the-job program at a sterile compounding pharmacy focused on compounding processes and procedures.[22]

There may be additional legislation by the state of Texas when its legislature is next in session. The Drug Quality and Security Act was passed 5 months after the 2013 regular session came to a close. By law, the Texas legislature meets in regular session on the second Tuesday in January of each odd-numbered year. This means the next session starts on January 13, 2015. Under the Texas constitution, the regular session of the Texas legislature is limited to 140 days. Interestingly, the State Senate is lead by the lieutenant governor, who is elected by the voters. The Speaker of the House is elected by the House members, or his or her peers. Only the governor can call a special session, a session of 30 days or less to address a governor-specific issue or piece of legislation. In most other states, the state legislatures can call themselves into a special session. Not in Texas![23] Although the specifics are not known at press time, it is hoped that the legislation will address pharmacy compounding.

SUMMARY

The path to H.R. 3204 and the Drug Quality and Security Act began with the FDA Modernization Act of 1997. It was a well-intentioned act, yet included a clause in Section 503A that would be determined to be unconstitutional and throw the compounding industry into confusion for more than a decade.

The path to create and pass a law in the United States is convoluted and akin to making sausage. It is important to have a sponsor for a bill that has a powerful position and a vested interest in the bill itself. Representative Fred Upton became the sponsor for H.R. 3204. He is the chairman of the House Committee on Energy and Commerce, which has principal responsibility over matters relating to health care, energy, the environment, consumer safety, telecommunications, commerce, manufacturing, and trade. He is also a representative in Michigan, the hardest-hit state by the NECC tragedy.

The definitions involving compounding vary by state and person within the industry. There are definitions for traditional compounding, compound manufacturing, and compounding for office use. What is not clear is the line between compound manufacturing and compounding for office use.

Several states have passed legislation to fill in the gaps or fix issues they know exist in regulating and providing oversight for compounding pharmacies. We looked at Massachusetts (where NECC was located), Michigan (the hardest-hit state in terms of infections and deaths from the fungal meningitis outbreak), California (always quick to attend a regulation party, but surprisingly recognized by some experts as a thought-leader in pharmaceutical drug regulation), Florida (in the past a troubled state, but recently doing great things in pharmaceutical drug regulation), and Texas (a great state that balances being business-friendly with smart regulation).

Representative Fred Upton described the intentions for the bill well when he introduced H.R. 3204 on September 27, 2013. He said, "My colleagues on both sides of the aisle on the committee and in the Senate have been relentless in their pursuit of the facts behind last year's deadly meningitis outbreak and working to prevent any such tragedy from happening again.... Michigan has been the hardest hit by the meningitis outbreak, and the sad truth is it could have been stopped. To all the families who have lost loved ones and to those patients who continue to suffer, we say 'never again.'"[24] Representative Fred Upton did a masterful job in getting a bipartisan bill passed in a very partisan Congress to address a bad situation. However, there is a lot of white space in the bill, and potentially unintended consequences of some of the language (or lack thereof) in key areas of pharmaceutical compounding. Let's start by taking a deeper dive into pharmacy compounding and the Drug Quality and Security Act.

ENDNOTES

1. Ramsey Cox, Senate Starts Work on Compound Drug Bill, The Hill, 2013, http://thehill.com/blogs/floor-action/senate/190036-senate-starts-work-on-compound-drug-bill.
2. *FDA Backgrounder*, November 21, 1997; http://www.fda.gov/RegulatoryInformation/Legislation/FederalFoodDrugandCosmeticActFDCAct/SignificantAmendmentstotheFDCAct/FDAMA/ucm089179.htm.
3. *Thompson v. Western States Medical Center*, Legal Information Institute, Cornell University, http://www.law.cornell.edu/supct/html/01-344.ZS.html; http://media.okstate.edu/faculty/jsenat/jb3163/thompsonexcerpts.html.

4. FDA's Compliance Policy Guide Regarding Compounding Pharmacy, 2002, http://democrats.energycommerce.house.gov/sites/default/files/documents/FDA-Compliance-Policy-Guide-for-Compounding-Pharmacy-2002-7-30.pdf.

5. Jeff N. Gibbs and Jennifer B. Davis, Fifth Circuit Medical Center Pharmacy v. Mukasey Decision Creates Circuit Split over FDCA § 503A Pharmacy Compounding "Safe Harbor," FDA Law Blog, 2008, http://www.fdalawblog.net/fda_law_blog_hyman_phelps/2008/07/fifth-circuit-m.html.

6. Syllabus, *Thompson, Secretary of Health and Human Services et al. v. Western States Medical Center et al.*, http://www.fda.gov/downloads/Drugs/GuidanceCompliance-RegulatoryInformation/PharmacyCompounding/UCM155167.pdf.

7. Text of Drug Quality and Security Act, GovTrack, https://www.govtrack.us/congress/bills/113/hr3204/text.

8. H.R. 3204—Drug Quality and Security Act, Congress.gov, https://www.congress.gov/bill/113th-congress/house-bill/3204.

9. http://www.michigan.gov/ag/0,4534,7-164-46849_47203-328315—,00.html.

10. Regulatory Information, FDA, http://www.fda.gov/RegulatoryInformation/Legislation/FederalFoodDrug andCosmeticActFDCAct/SignificantAmendmentstotheFDCAct/FDAMA/ucm089179.htm.

11. Ibid.

12. http://www.pccarx.com/what-is-compounding; http://www.fda.gov/Drugs/GuidanceComplianceRegulatoryInformation/PharmacyCompounding/ucm339764.htm.

13. Gov. Patrick Signs Compounding Pharmacy Oversight Bill, CBS Boston, 2014, http://boston.cbslocal.com/2014/07/10/gov-patrick-signs-compounding-pharmacy-oversight-bill/.

14. Steve LeBlanc, Mass. Lawmakers Pass Compounding Pharmacy Bill, CBS Boston, 2014, http://boston.cbslocal.com/2014/06/30/lawmakers-weigh-compounding-pharmacy-bill/.

15. http://www.misenategop.com/readarticle.asp?id=6686&District=22.

16. Chris Gautz, State Legislation Would Tighten Controls on Compounding Pharmacies, *Crain's Detroit Business*, 2014, http://www.crainsdetroit.com/print/article/20140427/NEWS/304279971/state-legislation-would-tighten-controls-on-compounding-pharmacies.

17. SB-294 Sterile Drug Products, California Legislative Information, http://leginfo.legislature.ca.gov/faces/billNavClient.xhtml?bill_id=201320140SB294.

18. Akerman's Health Law Rx Blog, http://www.akerman.com/Blogs/HealthLawRx/post/2014/05/09/Florida-Board-of-Pharmacy-Clarifies-that-Pharmacies-Cant-Compound-Sterile-Human-Drugs-for-Office-Use.aspx; phone call with Florida State Board of Pharmacy, September 26, 2014.

19. State Board Pharmacy, Colorado.gov, http://cdn.colorado.gov/cs/Satellite?c=Page&childpagename=DORA-Reg/DORALayout&cid=1251632324357&pagename=CBONWrapper.

20. Pharmacies Compounding Drugs for Hospitals, Colorado Legislative Council Staff Fiscal Note, 2014, http://statebillinfo.com/bills/fiscal/14/SB095_f2.pdf.

21. https://www.tshp.org/uploads/2/9/1/1/2911890/compounding_sterile_preps_-_tshp.pdf.

22. Ibid.

23. Phone call with an aide to Speaker of the House Joe Strauss, September 30, 2014.

24. Upton Statement on Introduction of H.R. 3204 the Drug Quality and Security Act, Energy & Commerce Committee, 2013, http://energycommerce.house.gov/press-release/upton-statement-introduction-hr-3204-drug-quality-and-security-act.

2

The World of Human Drug Compounding: Hope and Change

WHAT IS PHARMACY COMPOUNDING?

We gave a quick definition of *pharmacy compounding* in Chapter 1. In this chapter, we do a deeper analysis of what is pharmacy compounding. According to the Professional Compounding Centers of America (PCCA), *pharmacy compounding* is defined as follows:

> Pharmacy compounding is the art and science of preparing personalized medications for patients. Compounded medications are "made from scratch"—individual ingredients are mixed together in the exact strength and dosage form required by the patient. This method allows the compounding pharmacist to work with the patient and the prescriber to customize a medication to meet the patient's specific needs.[1]

Examples of pharmacy compounding are changing a medication from a solid pill to a liquid, changing or eliminating a nonessential ingredient in a medication due to allergies, or specifying exact dose(s) for both the active pharmaceutical ingredient and a specific patient. Sometimes pharmacy compounding is done to change the texture of the drug or add flavors to a medication. (Did you ever chew a pharmaceutical drug? Yuck!)

Sterile compounding is most common in the form of intravenous medications. Many groups perform the compounding of medications into intravenous medications, including hospital pharmacists, retail pharmacists, and privately owned compounding pharmacies.

When drugs are modified for individual patients, the process is known as traditional compounding. In its simplest form, traditional compounding may involve reformulating a drug, for example, by removing an inert ingredient or preservative due to a patient allergy. It may also involve making an alternative dosage form in a liquid suppository for a child or elderly patient who has difficulty swallowing a tablet.[2]

According to industry experts, a shortage of specific drugs and rising costs have combined to increase the reliance of hospitals on large-scale compounding pharmacies to meet their regular and repeatable needs for intravenous and sterile-injectable medication. The bulk production of regular and repeatable compounded drugs is known as compounding for office use (non-patient specific). This shift to large-scale compounding pharmacies not only increases economies of scale, but also increases patient exposure to risk if proper safety controls are not followed.

A LOOK AT COMPOUNDED DRUGS/MEDICATIONS

Example of Nonsterile, Traditional Compounding

A quick check of traditional pharmacies (Walmart, CVS, Walgreens, Target, etc.) confirms that sterile compounding is virtually outsourced to compound manufacturers and compounding pharmacies. A few of the local pharmacies (i.e., 24/7 pharmacies) do some nonsterile medication compounding with creams, capsules, and troches. Examples of these nonsterile compounded drugs are hormone replacement drugs and diaper rash creams. Since I have an 18-month-old grandson, let's take a look at an example of diaper rash creams.

Sometimes diaper rash can be really problematic, so much so that common over-the-counter products (such as A&D Ointment) don't remedy the problem. Some pharmacists use the prescription drug cholestyramine (commonly called Questran) to take the treatment of diaper rash to a higher level. Questran is primarily used to lower cholesterol levels, prevent coronary heart disease, and applicable to diaper rash, treat severe itching caused by liver disease. Its drug class is bile acid sequestrant,

Mode of Action Aquaphor

Builds a protective barrier
Keeps skin's own moisture
Creates an ideal healing environment

Allows the outflow
of excess fluid and
the inflow of oxygen

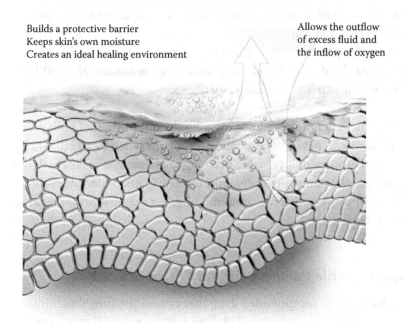

FIGURE 2.1
How Aquaphor works. (From Theresa Weber, Director, U.S. R&D, Derma Brands, Beiersdorf, May 22, 2014. With permission.)

which includes other drugs, such as colestipol, colesevelam, colesevelam hydrochloride, and colestipol hydrochloride.[3]

Aquaphor Healing Ointment is made by Eucerin, a division of Beiersdorf, Inc. It is an over-the-counter ointment designed to protect dry, cracked, or irritated skin to help enhance the natural healing process and restore smooth, healthy skin. Aquaphor is used to help heal raw, irritated skin caused by radiation treatments, facial resurfacing procedures, minor burns, eczema, and winter weather.[4]

According to Dr. Theresa Weber, the director of U.S. R&D, Derma Brands for Beiersdorf, the benefits of Aquaphor make it an ideal compounding base for topical preparations. In fact, these benefits extend beyond its role as a drug carrier. According to Dr. Weber, Aquaphor supports the skin in a number of ways to create an ideal wound-healing environment. She cites the following chemical and physical properties that help enable these benefits (Figure 2.1):

- It is miscible with both hydrophilic and lipophilic drugs.
- It is a skin protectant that shields skin from external irritants.
- Its semiocclusive nature retains essential skin moisture but allows excess fluid to escape.
- Its oxygen permeability allows oxygen to reach the wound.
- Essential lipids (fatty acids and cholesterol in lanolin alcohol) help restore the skin's protective barrier.[5]

The placement of Questran into Aquaphor brings the best of both products together to help address problematic diaper rashes. I can tell you by experience that when diaper rashes become problematic, it makes both the little ones and the parents/grandparents extremely uncomfortable! This is a simple example of nonsterile compounding, but one that brings relief to patients in need.

Example of Sterile Compounding for Office Use

Let's go back to the compounded drug that caused the fungal meningitis outbreak in 2012. The compounded drug was an epidural steroid injection (ESI). According to WebMD, an ESI is a combination of a corticosteroid with a local anesthetic pain relief medicine. Corticosteroids are strong anti-inflammatory medicines that are similar to natural hormones produced in the body that help control many necessary functions. Corticosteroids help relieve swelling and inflammation, taking pressure off nerves and other soft tissues that cause pain.

Because corticosteroid medicines take time to work, the local anesthetic medicine helps provide the patient immediate pain relief. The ESI is injected into the epidural space, or the space around the spinal cord and nerve roots. (Figure 2.2 shows a spine from the Southwest Scoliosis Center.) Patients usually receive short-term (2–3 weeks) relief from their pain through the use of ESIs.[6]

It is my understanding that hundreds of thousands of patients have benefited from ESIs. However, for the 14,000 people who received the tainted doses, the 751 people who were infected, and the 64 people who died, I would question the word *relief* in the definition. The fact is that it *should* have been safe if the drug was compounded in a sterile environment under 797 standard current good manufacturing practices (cGMP).

FIGURE 2.2
The human spine: example. (From Southwest Scoliosis Institute and Michael O'Brien. With permission.)

The ESI compounded drug was packaged and marketed by the New England Compounding Center (NECC), a compounding pharmacy in Framingham, Massachusetts. As I mentioned earlier, the tainted ESI doses were distributed to 75 medical facilities in 23 states. NECC was an example of a compounding pharmacy producing a drug product or medicine for office use and not specific patients.

Summary

These two examples have clear distinctions between traditional compounding to fill a specific patient need and compounding for office use. The issue is that there are so many drugs and so many variations that the combinations are almost exponential. It is easy to see why legislators defer decisions to sort out the definitions (and oversight) of all the compounded drugs to the Food and Drug Administration (FDA) and state boards of pharmacy. Let's take a look at what they did pass with the new law.

DRUG QUALITY AND SECURITY ACT*

There are two sections or titles in the H.R. 3204 Drug Quality and Security Act:

- Title I: Compounding Quality Act
- Title II: Drug Supply Chain Security Act

In this chapter, we focus on Title I: Compounding Quality Act, and the act that the Drug Quality and Security Act amended.

FOOD AND DRUG MODERNIZATION ACT OF 1997 AND 503A REVISITED

As we discussed in Chapter 1, the Drug Quality and Security Act amended the Federal Food, Drug, and Cosmetic Act (FFDCA) with respect to the regulation of compounding drugs. Section 127 of the FDA Modernization Act of 1997 (FDAMA) added Section 503A to the FFDCA, exempting compounded drugs from new drug laws as long as the compounded drug met several conditions/restrictions. Included in the exemptions were the myriad and lengthy new drug requirements (FDA trials, etc.), labeling requirements (the information/labeling on and with the manufacturer's bottle that a pharmacy normally gets and that the consumers would get if they got the prepackaged manufactured drug, e.g., a nasal spray in the manufacturer's box or a birth control packet), and the requirement that the compounded drugs had to be produced using cGMP. These exemptions were well intentioned, but left a lot of gaps and unanswered questions for compounding pharmacies.

---

* The following is summarized from multiple sources, with the two primary sources being www.congress.gov and www.fda.gov. Please take special note that the provisions of this act are continuously changing and being updated. If any of my readers have specific questions that are compliance related, please contact the FDA or your state board of pharmacy.

FDA TRIALS: WHY EXEMPTIONS ARE A BIG DEAL*

The FDA trials process for new drugs can take years and are very expensive. The following is a high-level snapshot of the process, as defined by the FDA. I say high-level because the journey to FDA approval for every new drug may have a path all its own.

1. Investigational new drug application. The pharmaceutical drug company and its partners may perform preclinical testing on animals and how the drug will be used with humans. The FDA will decide, based on the results submitted to it, if the new drug is reasonably safe to start testing on humans.
2. Phases 1 and 2 testing. Phase 1 testing is performed on healthy volunteers. Phase 2 testing begins if Phase 1 testing does not result in unacceptable toxicity. The number of Phase 2 volunteers is limited to approximately 300.
3. Phase 3 testing. If the results of Phase 2 are positive, Phase 3 begins. The number of Phase 3 subjects ranges from a few hundred to 3,000. At the end of Phase 3, the FDA will conduct a review to assess the new product's safety, efficacy, or optimal use.
4. New drug application (NDA). Assuming the FDA's review is positive, the pharmaceutical drug company (or a drug sponsor) will initiate a new drug application (NDA). This includes all animal and human data and analyses of the data, as well as information about how the drug behaves in the body and how it is manufactured. Assuming the application is complete, the average response time by the FDA to the NDA is 10 months, or 6 months for priority drugs.[7]

For pharmacies compounding drugs, the FDA trials process for every compounded drug would be so expensive and so time-consuming that only the highest-volume and highest-valued drugs would end up going through the process. A number of compounding pharmacies would elect to exit the business, and drug shortages would result for patients in need of medication. This is the opposite result that both the lawmakers and the FDA hope for from the Drug Quality and Safety Act. Thus, the

---

* The above description of the FDA trials process is a high-level snapshot. For a detailed review of the process itself, I urge my readers to visit the FDA website at http://www.fda.gov/drugs/resourcesforyou/consumers/ucm143534.htm or call the FDA and speak to one of the FDA trials specialists.

exemption from the FDA trials process (assuming certain conditions are met) is a big deal.

TITLE I: PHARMACY COMPOUNDING AND 503B

The Drug Quality and Security Act created a new section, 503B. In this section, a compounding pharmacy can elect to become an outsourcing facility. As stated before, an outsourcing facility can now qualify for exemptions from the FDA new drug approval requirements and labeling requirements. Outsourcing facilities are now subject to the cGMP requirements, whereas before they were more than likely considered pharmacies and considered exempt from them. They will now be inspected by the FDA according to a risk-based schedule in addition to the aforementioned reporting of adverse events.

This new law continues to exempt compounded drugs from new drug requirements, labeling requirements, and the forthcoming track and trace requirements under certain conditions. These new conditions are as follows: the drug/medication must be compounded by or under direct supervision of a licensed pharmacist, the drug/medication must be compounded in a registered outsourcing facility, and the drug/medication must meet other applicable requirements.[8] It also must be noted that the Drug Quality and Security Act mandates that outsourcing compounding pharmacies must be in compliance with the FDA's cGMP.

Outsourcing Facility Registration and Reporting

The Drug Quality and Security Act establishes an annual registration requirement for any outsourcing facility. Under the new law, compounding pharmacies that compound sterile drugs are now allowed to register with the FDA as an outsourcing facility. Once registered (and of course the fees are paid), an outsourcing facility must then meet certain conditions, as stated earlier, in order to be exempt from the Food, Drug, and Cosmetic Act's approval requirements and the requirement to label products with adequate directions for use. In addition to the aforementioned conditions, the outsourcing facility must also report specific information about the products that it compounds, including a list of all of the products it compounded during the previous 6 months, to the secretary of Health and Human Services (HHS). In addition to information about the compounded products, such as the source of the ingredients used to compound, the outsourcing facility must meet other conditions described in the new law. These conditions include the reporting of adverse events and labeling compounded products with certain information.[9]

Okay, so what happens to the information in these reports? This law requires the secretary of HHS to publish a list of drugs that present demonstrable difficulties for compounding that are reasonably likely to lead to an adverse effect on the safety or effectiveness of the drug, taking into account the risk and benefits to patients. It also requires the secretary to convene an advisory committee on compounding before creating the list, assess an annual establishment fee on each outsourcing facility, and as necessary, assess a reinspection fee.[10]

The information flow is bidirectional between the FDA, the secretary, and the state boards of pharmacy. The act requires the secretary to receive submissions from state boards of pharmacy describing any disciplinary actions taken against compounding pharmacies or any recall of a compounded drug, and expressing concerns that a compounding pharmacy may be violating the FFDCA. The secretary is required to establish a mechanism to receive submissions from state boards of pharmacy concerning certain actions taken against compounding pharmacies or expressing concerns that a compounding pharmacy may be acting contrary to Section 503A. This section is to be implemented in consultation with the National Association of Boards of Pharmacy (NABP). In addition, state boards of pharmacy must be notified when the secretary receives certain state submissions or makes a determination that a compounding pharmacy is acting contrary to Section 503A.[11]

To tighten up the restrictions on compounding pharmacies, this act prohibits the resale of a compounded drug labeled "not for resale," or the intentional falsification of a prescription for a compounded drug. It also deems a compounded drug to be misbranded if its advertising or promotion is false or misleading in any way.[12]

To help correct the Fifth Circuit/Ninth Circuit confusion described in Chapter 1, this act removed the unconstitutional provisions and repealed the prohibitions on advertising and promotion of compounded drugs by compounding pharmacies and repealed the requirement that prescriptions filled by a compounding pharmacy be unsolicited. This act also removed the uncertainty regarding the validity of Section 503A, which will be applicable to compounders nationwide.[13]

Last but not least, this act requires the comptroller general (Government Accountability Office (GAO)) to report on pharmacy compounding and the adequacy of state and federal efforts to ensure the safety of compounded drugs.[14]

TRADITIONAL COMPOUNDING

So what happened to pharmacies that do traditional compounding? Drugs produced by compounders that are not registered as outsourcing facilities must meet the conditions of Section 503A to qualify for the exemptions specified in that section. Even if the conditions of Section 503A are met, the compounded drugs are only exempt from those provisions of the FFDCA listed above. All other applicable provisions of the FFDCA remain in effect for compounded drugs, even if the conditions in Section 503A are met. For example, a compounded drug cannot be contaminated or made under unsanitary conditions, as was the case with the New England Compounding Center. And if a compounded drug does not qualify for the exemptions under either Section 503A or 503B (see below) of the FFDCA, the compounded drug would be subject to all of the requirements of the FFDCA that are applicable to drugs made by conventional manufacturers, including the new drug approval and adequate directions for use requirements. The FDA assumes that compounding pharmacies that only perform traditional compounding will fall under the oversight of state boards of pharmacy.[15]

Under the new section, 503B, a compounding pharmacy can elect to become an outsourcing facility. As stated before, an outsourcing facility can now qualify for exemptions from the FDA new drug approval requirements and labeling requirements. Outsourcing facilities are now subject to the cGMP requirements, whereas before they were more than likely considered pharmacies and considered exempt from this requirement. They will now be inspected by the FDA according to a risk-based schedule in addition to the aforementioned reporting of adverse events and information on the drugs they are compounding.[16]

AND WE HAVE LIFTOFF—MAYBE

If nothing changes by the time readers read this chapter, compounding pharmacies can elect to become outsourcing facilities under 503B, register with the FDA as an outsourcing facility, and market/advertise their compounded medications to hospitals, medical facilities, and health care providers. The doctors and patients can purchase these compounded drugs, knowing that they were compounded in outsourcing facilities subject to cGMP requirements and federal oversight by licensed pharmacists under state oversight.

Compounding pharmacies that do not elect to become outsourcing facilities or register with the FDA will still be subject to FFDCA requirements. They may be considered manufacturers and subject to FDA new drug approval requirements and labeling requirements. These compounding pharmacies are also anticipated to be under the oversight of the state boards of pharmacy.[17]

ISSUES TO BE RESOLVED

The Title I regulations are still being drafted. Progress has been made to address the regulatory gaps in the compounding of drugs. However, there are numerous issues that still need to be resolved. In my opinion, there needs to be a uniform standard to define which drugs fall under pharmacy compounding and which drugs are considered in the manufacturing or compounding for office use category. We will discuss the issue of inspections of facilities, which keeps coming up in both the Drug Quality and Security Act and the states' responses. Compounding pharmacies and manufacturers need to know who will be doing the inspections, how often these inspections will take place, and what organization will do the accreditation of the inspectors. (We discuss inspections in Chapter 3.) In addition, the question on everyone's mind is, who will pay for these inspections? Another issue is transparency. Two compounding pharmacy owners I spoke with had opposite opinions on this issue. One said he wanted the inspections to remain private. This way, if there are issues uncovered, his team has a chance to fix them without the issues becoming public knowledge. The other pharmacy owner said she hopes all inspections become public knowledge because we are all human and mistakes can happen. The real test is how a compounding pharmacy responds to inspection findings and fixes the issues once they have been identified through proper policies and procedures.

Regarding the NECC, inspections were not necessarily the problem but enforcement was a big problem. Neither the FDA nor the state agencies took action when it was apparent action was necessary. As such, compounding pharmacies and manufacturers are now wondering which agencies (federal and state) can and will take action when violations occur. They also need to know the penalties for violations, up to and including the closure of their facilities. Another big issue was the absence of governance and leadership with the NECC. Unfortunately, governance and leadership cannot be regulated. Let's take a look at both in terms of the Drug Quality and Security Act.

GOVERNANCE AND LEADERSHIP

My definition of *governance* for compounding pharmacies is to conduct the actions and affairs of their companies, which includes the processes, procedures, and expectations regarding patient care, compliance to all federal and state laws and regulations, financial risk, and the culture-based setting of incentives. These incentives can be positive or negative, depending on the behavior and actions of the leaders. I would expect the governing board (most likely a board of directors) to set a commitment to quality for compounded medicines for patients, including a continuous quality improvement process that allows for systemic learning for the compounding pharmacy. This continuous quality improvement process should embrace both the compounding pharmacy's customers and suppliers, and be embedded into the compounding pharmacy's strategic plan.

My definition of *leadership* for compounding pharmacies is the actions of the senior executives to develop the vision, strategic plan, and operating plan for their companies within the boundaries set by the board of directors. Leadership should include the operating objectives, goals, and operating strategies that align with the board's expectations regarding patient care, compliance to all federal and state laws and regulations, the management of risk, and the implementation of incentives and penalties for

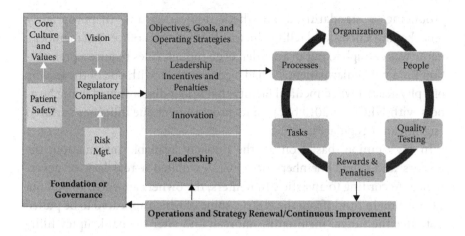

FIGURE 2.3
Governance and leadership. (From Fred A. Kuglin.)

results. The employees of a compounding pharmacy should be involved to identify their tasks and activities that support and align with the vision and strategic plan established by the senior executives and approved by the company's governing board.

In my first book, *Customer-Centered Supply Chain Management: A Link-by-Link Guide*, I used an exhibit that connected the foundation or board strategy with "transformation design" for the leadership team and an implementation approach for the managers and employees. Figure 2.3 is an adaptation of my exhibit.

GOVERNANCE, LEADERSHIP, AND THE NECC

If the NECC had established proper governance and leadership, the tasks, processes, organization, people, quality testing, and rewards and penalties would have been aligned for all employees to do the right things. Something was definitely missing for many years in these areas.

The NECC had ample opportunities to exhibit proper governance and leadership and take appropriate action to fix issues within its facilities. According to the *New York Times*, the NECC had a series of complaints lodged against it over a number of years. For example, the Massachusetts State Health Department inspected NECC in 2006. In the same year, the FDA issued NECC a warning letter accusing the NECC of illegally producing a standardized anesthetic topical cream, inappropriately repackaging a drug, and telling doctors that using an office staff member's name was enough to put in an order, even though rules require a prescription for a particular patient.[18] I had a conversation with one of the leaders of a physician-owned medical facility that said it discontinued doing business with NECC in 2010 because its procurement due diligence surfaced "significant irregularities."

In my opinion, based on all the publicly available information, the owners and board members of NECC exhibited a real lack of governance. According to an article in Reuters, the owners appeared to pull out $16 million in funds from the NECC, some of which appeared to be pulled out after the fungal meningitis outbreak and after the bankruptcy filing by NECC. "The bottom line is that instead of using the money to remedy the pharmacy's problems, which now look like a ticking time bomb, they took the money out," said David Molton, a lawyer at Brown Rudnick LLP, which is representing the official committee of unsecured creditors in NECC's bankruptcy.[19] The actions of the owners do not align with patient safety or proper guidelines for the NECC senior executives.

Ultimately, the NECC's owners would pay a steep price. On July 15, 2014, a Massachusetts bankruptcy judge approved a $100 million settlement with NECC. Bill Baldiga, the managing director of Brown Rudnick's litigation and restructuring department, who led a team of the firm's attorneys to represent the creditors' committee and the victims, said, "The judge [U.S. bankruptcy court judge Henry J. Boroff] made findings that it was very much, if not, [the best solution]."[20]

The pain of the victims and their families is far from over. I am sure the lawsuits in many other states will go on for years against the owners and partners of NECC. How can you compensate someone infected by tainted medicine? More importantly, how do you compensate the families of those who died as a result of the tainted medicine?

I cannot speak for the owners and partners of NECC because I was not one of them or involved in any of the litigation. There are two sides to every story. However, from a governance standpoint, where was the cavalry when the first set of complaints, audit findings, and FDA warning letters were issued? Where was the corrective action, the independent audits, the replacement of the executive team, and all the other actions taken by good boards of directors when serious issues surface? Where was the leadership to set in motion the corrective action steps, inclusive of voluntary closing of facilities and recalls of suspected tainted medicines, when the first set of complaints surfaced? How many lives would have been saved if the executives took corrective action at the first signs of problems? How many infections could have been averted if the board provided proper governance and incentivized the right behavior of its executive team? The answers to these questions can range from none to all. I hope for the victims and their families that some of these answers were determined in the two years from the outbreak of the infections to the settlement.

Leaders are defined by how they guide companies through a crisis. I previously described how Johnson & Johnson responded to the Tylenol tampering—and it wasn't even an issue under their control! However, it involved patient safety and brand protection. Today, in a number of MBA schools, the Johnson & Johnson response to the Tylenol tampering is taught as a case study on how to properly lead a company through a crisis.

SUMMARY

We defined *pharmacy compounding* at a deeper level. We also showed examples of nonsterile compounding solutions and compounded medicines that are sterile for office use. We introduced the Drug Quality and Security Act and Title I: Compounding Quality Act, and proceeded to discuss the Food and Drug Modernization Act of 1997 as a prelude to the Drug Quality and Security Act. We quickly revisited Section 503A and went through why its exemptions (if earned and qualified) are so important by showing the extensive process of FDA trials for new drugs. We then looked at Section 503B and outsourcing facility registration and reporting.

We discussed some issues to be resolved, such as a few gray areas to be defined and inspections of compounding facilities. We then did an in-depth look at governance and leadership, and how there were breakdowns in these areas with the NECC.

Going back to my introduction, I mentioned that there are close to 2 million people employed in the pharmaceutical drug industry. People make mistakes. There are also people who do bad things, either by accident or intentionally. With the NECC, it appears that negligence and an absence of governance and leadership contributed to the fungal infections and loss of life. Regulations to compensate for bad governance and bad leadership will prevent bad situations from getting worse. There must be additional measures and innovations to prevent such situations from occurring. In Chapter 3, we review the compounding supply chain and ways to help prevent another NECC from occurring.

ENDNOTES

1. What Is Compounding? PCCA, http://www.pccarx.com/what-is-compounding/ what-is-compounding.
2. Examining Drug Compounding, FDA, http://www.fda.gov/NewsEvents/Testimony/ ucm353654.htm.
3. Questran, WebMD, http://www.webmd.com/drugs/drug-3334-Questran+Oral. aspx?drugid=3334.
4. Aqua for Healing Ointment, Eucerin, https://www.eucerinus.com/products/ aquaphor/aquaphor-healing-ointment.html.
5. Theresa Weber, Director of U.S. R&D, Derma Brands for Beiersdorf, email, May 22, 2014.
6. Epidural Steroid Injections for Lumbar Spinal Stenosis, WebMD, http://www. webmd.com/back-pain/epidural-steroid-injections-for-lumbar-spinal-stenosis.
7. The FDA's Drug Review Process: Ensuring Drugs Are Safe and Effective, FDA, http://www.fda.gov/drugs/resourcesforyou/consumers/ucm143534.htm.
8. H.R. 3204—Drug Quality and Security Act, Library of Congress, http://beta.congress. gov/bill/113th-congress/house-bill/3204.
9. Compounding, FDA, http://www.fda.gov/drugs/GuidanceComplianceRegulatory- Information/PharmacyCompounding/.
10. Ibid.
11. Ibid.
12. Ibid.
13. Ibid.
14. Ibid.
15. Outsourcing, FDA Implementation of the Compounding Quality Act, FDA, http://www.fda.gov/Drugs/GuidanceComplianceRegulatoryInformation/ PharmacyCompounding/ucm375804.htm#Outsourcing.
16. Compounding, FDA, http://www.fda.gov/drugs/GuidanceComplianceRegulatory- Information/PharmacyCompounding/.
17. Frequently Asked Questions about Pharmaceutical Compounding, APhA, http://www.pharmacist.com/frequently-asked-questions-about-pharmaceuti- cal-compounding.
18. Denise Grady et al., Scant Oversight of Drug Maker in Fatal Meningitis Outbreak, *The New York Times*, 2012, http://www.nytimes.com/2012/10/07/us/scant-drug- maker-oversight-in-meningitis-outbreak.html?pagewanted=2&_r=0.
19. Tim McLaughin, Creditors Probe Meningitis-Linked Pharmacy Owners' Pay, *Reuters*, 2013, http://www.reuters.com/article/2013/01/22/us-usa-health-meningitis- idUSBRE90L0GS20130122.
20. Jessica Bartlett, Judge Affirms $100 Million Settlement with New England Compounding Center, *Boston Business Journal*, 2013, http://www.bizjournals.com/ boston/blog/health-care/2014/07/judge-affirms-100-million-settlement-with-new. html?page=all.

3

Pharmacy Compounding:
The Supply Chain World

PHARMACY COMPOUNDING SUPPLY CHAIN DEFINED

In Chapter 2, we defined *pharmacy compounding* using phrases such as "personalized medications for patients," "made from scratch," and "individual ingredients mixed together in the exact strength and dosage," etc. Let's focus on the supply chain, and how the new law will potentially impact participants in this supply chain.

A dear friend of mine, whom I believe is one of the best supply chain professionals I have met in my career, used to say, "It all begins with an order." He was almost right with his comment. It does all begin with an order—or in pharmacy compounding, a doctor's prescription—from customers/patients. Knowing the patient demand for compounded drugs provides the foundation for the planning of the supply chain.

There are three main parts to the pharmacy compounding supply chain: from doctor prescription/patient demand to ingredients, from ingredients to compounding pharmacies, and from compounding pharmacies to patients (Figure 3.1).

FROM PATIENT/DOCTOR PRESCRIPTION
TO INGREDIENTS

Supply chain professionals know that accumulating patient demand in an order management system is a key first step. A good order management system uses a solid bill of materials module to break down the patient

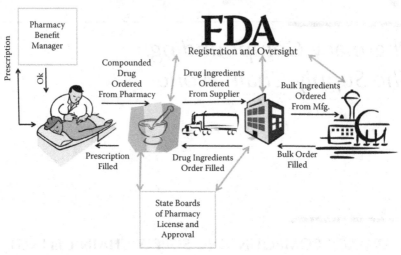

FIGURE 3.1
Pharmacy prescription order-fill process, compound medicines view.

demand into the needed ingredients or active pharmaceutical ingredients (APIs) and compounding ingredients. The result is an "ingredient need sheet" to be used with ingredient/chemical suppliers. How does this work in real life? There are a few companies that compete in this area. In my opinion, the Professional Compounding Centers of America (PCCA) showcases how this is properly done.

PCCA: Overview*

In 1981, an antinausea medication was discontinued by a pharmaceutical drug company. A physician challenged a Houston-area pharmacist to compound the medication for his patient. The pharmacist procured the necessary compounds to produce the needed medication. The prescription was a success. The pharmacist realized that there were many other pharmacists being challenged by physicians to produce compounded medications. This network of pharmacists, united by a commitment to meet patient needs, was the foundation of PCCA, which was incorporated in 1981.

---

* This is a summary of PCCA, based on a personal visit to their Houston headquarters, interviews with member compounding pharmacy owners, and public information. It is used with permission from PCCA.

Today, PCCA has become the independent compounding pharmacist's complete resource for pharmaceutical compounds, fine chemicals, equipment, devices, flavors, Accreditation Council for Pharmacy Education (ACPE)–accredited training and education, pharmacy software, marketing, business, and pharmacy consulting. Its membership includes more than 3,900 independent community pharmacists in the United States, Canada, Australia, and other countries around the world.

Order Aggregation and Supplier Sourcing

Because PCCA has more than 3,900 independent community pharmacists as its members, they have a critical mass to be able to capture the pharmacy demand (current and historical) for repeatable ingredients used in compounding and use it to forecast future demand. The ability to forecast future demand is critical to begin procurement operations.

The PCCA procurement group breaks down the forecasted demand into ingredients. It then employs a dual-sourcing strategy, making sure that there are at least two approved suppliers able to provide the needed APIs and compounding ingredients at all times. This is not as easy as it sounds, and is critical to meet the needs of patients.

The PCCA supplier sourcing strategy demands that suppliers of active pharmaceutical ingredients at a minimum are Food and Drug Administration (FDA) registered (as outlined in the Drug Quality and Security Act), have facilities that use current good manufacturing practices (cGMP) as outlined by the FDA, the Federal Food, Drug, and Cosmetic Act (FFDCA), and the Drug Quality and Security Act, and have been approved through PCCA's quality control and R&D departments. There are also complexities in the formulation and mixing of the compounded drugs, with the slightest of differences in supplier ingredients affecting the formulation and quality of the final drug.

Once suppliers successfully go through the supplier approval process (which includes price, quality expectations, and approved transportation providers), they are ready to start receiving specific orders from PCCA for APIs and compounding ingredients. The PCCA has suppliers all around the world, from the United States to China, and from India to Australia. Order lead times and quality control are a way of life to globally source these APIs and compounding ingredients.

Order Placement, Supplier Base Compound Shipment and PCCA Receipt

When orders are placed with approved suppliers, the process to physically make the needed APIs and compounding ingredients is initiated. Suppliers manufacture, package, and ship in accordance to their PCCA purchase orders. PCCA receives the supplier shipments in controlled environments (Figure 3.2).

All supplier shipments are tested by the PCCA quality control personnel, using a broad spectrum of criteria as dictated by PCCA's testing protocol. Only the APIs and compounding ingredients that pass the QC test are formally accepted and placed into inventory (Figures 3.3 and 3.4).

FIGURE 3.2
Raw chemicals await testing to verify quality and labeling. (From PCCA. With permission.)

FIGURE 3.3
Quality control testing of chemicals to determine potency and quality. (From PCCA. With permission.)

FIGURE 3.4
Approved chemicals are labeled and placed into the supply chain to await being repacked into smaller, more usable amounts. (From PCCA. With permission.)

FIGURE 3.5
Rejected chemicals are labeled, pulled out of the supply chain, and shipped back to the supplier. (From PCCA. With permission.)

According to PCCA personnel, 3% of all shipments fail the QC test and are refused.[1] Rejected shipments become part of supplier reviews and the contract renewal process (Figure 3.5).

The Drug Quality and Security Act

One major item to be determined is the track and trace requirement as dictated by the Drug Quality and Security Act. As of 2014, lawfully compounded drugs are exempt from the track and trace regulations, but not exempt from pedigree requirements.[2] The critical question is, where does the pedigree start? Does the pedigree have to start with the supplier in

India or China or Australia? Can the pedigree start with PCCA's receipt of APIs and compounding ingredients? PCCA already has a pedigree system as required by the state of Florida. Will this be sufficient, or will the Drug Quality and Security Act be changed? For now, we will have to wait for this item to be determined by the FDA. PCCA will have to be prepared to initiate the pedigree necessary to comply with the upcoming track and trace requirements if compounded drugs are not exempted. This should not be a big problem since they have a similar program to satisfy the state of Florida.

Compounding Pharmacy Order Fill

Member pharmacists place specific orders to PCCA for the APIs and compounding ingredients to make the compounded drugs needed by their patients. PCCA performs its order-fill activities and ships the material to its member customers. The PCCA process, from supplier approval to customer ship, is tightly controlled under cGMP guidelines. Continuous testing is done throughout the process to ensure the safety and security of drug compounds.

PCCA receives the orders from its member pharmacies, fills them, and most of the time ships the product within 24 hours of receipt of the order. There is a significant amount of interaction between PCCA and its member pharmacies on both orders and consultation regarding formulations. In fact, PCCA averages over 3,000 inquiries per day to its consultants from its member pharmacies.

The process from patient demand to shipment to the compounding pharmacy meets/exceeds the known requirements under the Drug Quality and Safety Act provisions. Why is this important? It is important because PCCA's market share with their independent pharmacy members is over 50%. If the intent of the lawmakers passing H.R. 3204 into law as the Drug Quality and Security Act was in part to secure the compounding pharmacy supply chain, they are over halfway there, from patient order demand to APIs and compounding ingredients, thanks to PCCA.

FROM APIS AND COMPOUNDING INGREDIENTS TO COMPOUNDED MEDICINES

During my research for this book, I had the pleasure of visiting four sterile compounding pharmacies in two states. All four owners expressed interest in remaining anonymous. In all four cases, the owners of these sterile compounding pharmacies believed they were *not* manufacturers, but pharmacies producing sterile drugs for doctors and patients. In my estimation, approximately 75% of all of their orders were for sterile, injectable drugs for patients "for office use" (i.e., scoliosis centers, medical facilities, etc.), and the remaining 25% were for sterile drugs tied to specific patient prescriptions.

Their receipt and inventory processes were all very similar. Supplier orders were received from the transport carrier in the morning, with the APIs and compounding ingredients unloaded from the truck and placed directly into inventory. Since all four happened to be PCCA members, they assumed that the received material was tested and packed in a sterile environment. I did witness other compounds being placed into a sterile inventory location that were bought from local sources (inert ingredients) and assumed to be sterile as well.

At two of the compounding pharmacies, I was present early enough to witness the arrival of the compounding pharmacists. These pharmacists would get ready for the day, and then proceed to sort their "to dos" into three parts: emergency orders to be filled right away for patients either directly through a physician or through a medical center, the rest of the direct patient orders, and the office use orders to replenish medical center inventories. I was able to observe the intensity of the pharmacists as they filled the emergency orders from behind glass windows.

At all times, there appeared to be great care to observe the rules for a sterile environment. For two compounding pharmacies, other on-duty pharmacists spot-checked the compounded drugs for quality and accuracy of the formulation. It was reassuring to see the dedication of these pharmacists to helping people/patients in need.

The Complication

In the United States, there are approximately 7,500 compounding pharmacies, with approximately 3,000 of these compounding pharmacies making sterile products.[3] My sampling of four compounding centers is a small sample, but it does illuminate the complexity of the safety and security issue.

It is apparent that pharmacists are focused on patient (and office) order fill. All four compounding pharmacies spoke about and focused on a sterile environment. However, I received a variety of opinions on what constituted a sterile environment. Thanks to my nephew Jeff, who received his PhD in biology, I adopted the following definition: "a sterile environment is one that is free of living organic material."[4] Not surprisingly, Biology Online has the following definition: "A sterile environment is an environment that lacks living organic material."[5] J.D. Willey, the general manager of Eagle Analytical Services, defines a sterile environment as "the total absence of microbial activity."[6]

In my introduction, I explained that people make pharmaceutical drugs, people transport and sell pharmaceutical drugs, and people consume pharmaceutical drugs. People are not bacteria-free. In fact, according to Carolyn Bohach, a microbiologist at the University of Idaho, along with other estimates from scientific studies, there are 10 times more bacterial cells in your body than human cells.[7] Most of these bacteria (I am told) are "good bacteria," with some of it "bad bacteria." Then how in the world is a sterile environment really free of living organic material if people work in a sterile environment to compound pharmaceutical drugs?

Part of the answer rests with all the precautions that pharmacists take to limit the bacteria being transmitted into the sterile environment. From the space suits to foot covering, the pharmacists I observed took extraordinary care to limit the exposure of bacteria to the environment. However, I did not see the cleaning (or sterilization) of the sterile environment, nor did I observe the emptying of the trash and medical waste left over from a day's worth of compounding drugs.

During my career, I had the pleasure of visiting semiconductor "clean rooms" and, for one top 10 hospital, a prototype of a sterile ICU room. The semiconductor clean rooms were very sophisticated, testing in real time the bacteria in the air as well as changes on any surface of the room. However, these clean rooms were also void of humans. In the sterile ICU room, I was able to view the monitors on the room during the proof-of-concept stage of the test. Contamination was detected during the room change by maintenance people fixing the equipment, during care by nurses transmitting bacteria first to the push plates on the doors and then to the door handle to the restroom (despite wearing gloves), and by the cleaning people not wearing proper shoe coverings when washing down the floors.

As such, the complication for the compounding pharmacies is having pharmacists compound drugs in a sterile environment using sterile and other drugs, placing the drugs into vials and containers, and then placing the orders into their shipping boxes or totes that may or may not be sterile.

What of course counts is that the compounded medicine is sterile in the vial or container when the physician or nurse administers it to the patient.

Good Manufacturing Practices: The Foundation to Ensure a Safe and Sterile Environment

Earlier in the book I referred to current good manufacturing practices. So what exactly are good manufacturing practices? According to the FDA, good manufacturing practices are practices recommended by the FDA to authorize and control the licensing, manufacturing, and sale of pharmaceutical drugs and food products. These practices combine to provide the minimum requirements that (in our case) pharmaceutical compounding drug manufacturers and compounding pharmacies must meet to ensure that the compounded drugs do not pose a safety risk to patients and are of high quality.[8] The FDA's good manufacturing practices are extensive in nature. There is a whole process to be GMP certified with the FDA (and it could be an entire book unto itself).

Using information from the FDA website[8] and input received from several calls with FDA representatives, I have developed a list of foundational principles that GMP evolve around:

- Controlled environmental conditions to prevent cross-contamination of a pharmaceutical compounding drug product with other drug or proscribed material that may cause the compounded drug to be unsafe for consumption and a risk to patients. (This is an area in which the New England Compounding Center (NECC) apparently failed. It is also an area that should have been a top priority for the FDA and the Massachusetts Board of Pharmacy because many officials have cited the presence of a cardboard recycling center in close proximity to the NECC compounding facility as a potential hazard. Used cardboard has a high propensity to absorb moisture and bacteria.)
- Cleanliness. Compounding pharmacies and manufacturers must maintain a clean, sanitized manufacturing and compounding area.
- Process mapping and process modeling of the entire compound manufacturing and compounding processes. These processes must be clearly defined to employees and supply chain partners. They must also be validated vis-à-vis the compounded product specifications (as PCCA does with its suppliers). This can be a huge job to keep current!

- The compounding pharmacy and compounding manufacturing processes must also be controlled through a compounding pharmacy's policies and procedures. These policies and procedures must be written in such a manner that they are understood by people like you and me. Some industry people refer to this as good documentation practices. (There is always a tendency for technical people such as PhDs and MDs to write and talk with techno-speak.) Any process changes must be evaluated and validated accordingly. In addition, compounding pharmacy manufacturers must have someone identified to document and enforce the policies and procedures.
- These good documentation practices call for records to be made (automatically done or performed manually) during the compounding/manufacturing processes to make sure the process steps and the related policies and procedures are followed. Any deviations (i.e., quantity, quality, specifications, etc.) must be documented and investigated.
- The records produced during the compound manufacturing and compounding processes are to be used to create a history of the batch of compounded drugs. This history must be available and accessible when needed.
- A drug recall program must be defined and communicated so that any batch of drugs can be removed from the supply chain quickly and efficiently (including point of sale or use), utilizing the compounding records mentioned above.
- From the time a drug is compounded until the final point of use/consumption by a patient, the distribution process must minimize the risk to the quality and condition of the drug. This includes packaging, protective shipping containers, and proper shipping and receiving procedures.
- Compounding pharmacies and compound manufacturers must have a complaint management process that includes receiving complaints, investigating any quality defects, taking appropriate measures to address the causes of the quality defects and prevent the defects from occurring again, and documenting every complaint received and handled.[9]

In June 2014, I spoke with an FDA representative who informed me that a pharmaceutical drug or compounded drug can pass all specifications tests but be deemed "adulterated" because the drug was manufactured or compounded in a facility that was determined not to comply with cGMP.

As such, pharmacy manufacturing and pharmacy compounding companies must comply with cGMP.[10]

Are We There Yet?

As a dad and a new grandpa, this is a frequently heard phrase on family trips. It is a very appropriate phrase for the journey to the Drug Quality and Security Act. Pharmacy compounding manufacturers and pharmacy compounding facilities are currently at a loss on what agency will audit them and what specific audit guidelines will be used. One owner of a compounding pharmacy that has three locations (two sterile compounding facilities and one nonsterile compounding facility) commented: "We just need to know the guidelines and the rules so we can be compliant. I wish I could use the money I am spending in legal fees toward helping get the compounded drugs to patients in need."

One Best Practice to Model

For several years I worked for Frito-Lay, which is owned by PepsiCo. When I was responsible for supply chain facilities, we utilized the services of the American Institute of Baking (AIB), or AIB International. AIB provides food safety inspections, audits, and certifications, food safety education, and research and technical services.[11] Frito-Lay at the time contracted for quarterly audits of all manufacturing and warehouse facilities. These audits were both scheduled and unscheduled. The AIB auditors used FDA guidelines as a basis to develop their audit templates. They were very professional, knowledgeable, and engaging in transferring knowledge on both the whats and whys behind every audit point. However, Frito-Lay executives demanded guidelines above and beyond the FDA guidelines for these audits. The AIB audits reflected these stricter guidelines.

One time we had an unannounced visit by the FDA. An auditor called one hour before arriving at one of our facilities. When he arrived, we welcomed him, brought him to the conference room, gave him a cup of coffee, and provided him with copies of our AIB audits for the past year. We proceeded to discuss with him our challenges, and brought in the people who were instrumental in maintaining a food-safe environment and addressing any findings that were identified in the AIB audits. He proceeded to do his audit, came back with "all is well," and was on his way.

We all knew that when we passed an AIB audit, we would easily pass an FDA audit. We also knew that if we failed an AIB audit more than once, we were quickly looking for another job! I can tell you from personal experience that our preparation for an AIB audit was intense and ongoing. It was a pleasure to work for a company like Frito-Lay that took consumer safety so seriously and with such a professional organization as AIB International. Right now, compounding pharmacies are at an inflection point on what do to be prepared for upcoming audits with so many unknown variables. The following is one recommendation on how good compounding pharmacies can tackle this dilemma.

The Best Defense Is a Good Offense

Several state boards of pharmacy are also scrambling to figure out how and who will do the audits for compound manufacturing facilities that are truly manufacturers (should be the FDA) and all other compounding pharmacies (should be the state boards of pharmacy). The complications arise when these facilities reside in one state (such as NECC in Massachusetts) and the compounding pharmacies are in another state. There is a lot of hallway chatter in the state boards of pharmacy to work with their state legislators to pass legislation authorizing the use of out-of-state companies to perform the required audits. Some states have already done this, as we noted in Chapter 1. There are several firms—both industry firms and private equity groups—participating in these conversations to perform the out-of-state audits.

There is an opportunity for an existing firm such as PCCA (with potentially a nonprofit hospital group) to initiate an audit program similar to AIB's for all compounding pharmacies. These audits could be designed around the current and still emerging guidelines from the FDA and the guidelines set forth by the state boards of pharmacy. The key success factor is to audit to the highest standards of the FDA and the state boards of pharmacy. There are also additional governing agencies that need to be included, such as the Drug Enforcement Administration (DEA), but this will be covered in Chapter 8. These audits would be done on a subscription basis, and be available to regulators if and when their auditors request the audit findings.

There is also an opportunity for compounding pharmacies to use these audits with their "for office use" customers. Two large top 10 hospital systems I spoke with said they have extensive quality control reviews with compounding pharmacies before contracting out for compounding medicines. They both said if there was an independent audit organization used by the compounding pharmacies with FDA- and state agency–approved standards used for their audits, their quality reviews would be cut at least in half. Having such a service and producing audit results upon demand would be a great sales and marketing capability with prospective customers.

There are a lot of items that will need to be defined, such as the go-forward process if significant audit findings are discovered, the response times to audit findings, the sharing of the information from the audits, which could infringe on improper disclosure of proprietary information, etc. However, the companies that take the initiative to institute such a program should and would be held in high esteem by the regulators—as I found out first-hand with Frito-Lay, AIB International, and the FDA. As one senior executive of a big state board of pharmacy said on June 16, "Such a program would be awesome!"

Back to PCCA

Exclusive of cGMP but inclusive of drug quality and safety are two other groups of practices: good laboratory practices (GLP) and good clinical practices (GCP).

Good laboratory practices are defined as "regulations put in place in the 1970's that establish standards for the conduct and reporting of nonclinical laboratory studies and are intended to assure the quality and integrity of safety data submitted to FDA."[10] These regulations form a quality system of management controls for (in our case) compounding pharmacies and their supply chain partners to ensure the uniformity, consistency, reliability, reproducibility, quality, and integrity of chemical (including pharmaceuticals) nonclinical safety tests, from physiochemical properties through acute to chronic toxicity tests.[12]

Good clinical practices are defined as international ethical and scientific quality standards for the design, conduct, monitoring, recording, auditing, analysis, and reporting of studies. These standards ensure that the data reported are credible and accurate, and that subjects' rights and confidentiality are protected.[13] GCP are more applicable for clinical trials, so let's focus on GLP, as they relate to regulatory agency audits of compounding pharmacies.

Eagle Analytical Services

Eagle Analytical Services is a PCCA company that has served PCCA customers since 2004. For the compounding pharmacy members, Eagle Analytical Services performs tests on routine samples, fine-tunes formulations, and provides feedback on techniques. Eagle Analytical Services is also registered with the DEA and the Texas Department of Public Safety.

Eagle Analytical Services offers the highest quality in preparation testing for sterility, bacterial endotoxins, microbial detection, beyond-use dating (BUD) determination, and active ingredient potency. It uses state-of-the-art equipment, combined with the experience and knowledge of its team, to be a preferred testing partner for compounding pharmacies. What sets Eagle Analytical Services apart is how it works with compounding pharmacies when its tests produce unexpected results (Figure 3.6).[14]

One capability that sets Eagle Analytical Services apart from its competition is its ScanRDI* sterility test protocol used to detect microorganisms in sterile compounded preparations. All standard U.S. Pharmacopeia (USP) test organisms are detected, resulting in this test method meeting the requirements of USP 797 for the testing of sterile compounded preparations (Figure 3.7).[15]

The ScanRDI system uses a scanning laser cytometer that quickly detects viable microbial cells (amazingly down to one microorganism), without the need for an extended incubation period. This is critical when patient safety is at risk. This system also uses an analytical scan module, laser source, computer, microscope/camera with a motorized stage, and other associated equipment.

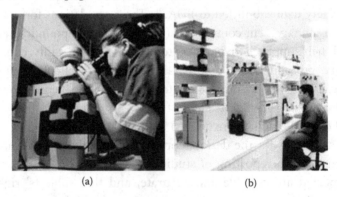

(a) (b)

FIGURE 3.6
(a) PCCA lab technician reviewing the product sent to Eagle. (b) Technician using the ScanRDI to test finished compounds sent to Eagle. (From Eagle Analytical Services. With permission.)

FIGURE 3.7
With its unique combination of speed and sensitivity, ScanRDI is crucial in microbial detection. (From Eagle Analytical Services. With permission.)

FIGURE 3.8
Dr. Zolner is reviewing lab results after completion of testing at Eagle Analytical Services. (From Eagle Analytical Services. With permission.)

The system is one thing, but the use of the system determines the quality of the reporting of the test results. Eagle Analytical Services performs a three-step procedure on all measurement runs to ensure the quality of its testing results. These steps are as follows: (1) a basic instrumentation performance and calibration test, (2) a zero control test, and (3) a positive control test. Eagle Analytical Services does not issue any reports until all three tests have been successfully run (Figure 3.8).[16]

PCCA and the AIB Industry Audit Solution for Compounding Pharmacies

PCCA, inclusive of its sister company Eagle Analytical Services, has a solid base to develop drug-safe audits for compounding pharmacies. These audits should be both scheduled and unscheduled, and incorporate the FDA and state board of pharmacy audit templates, current good manufacturing practices, and good laboratory practices. As mentioned before, a lot of particulars need to be defined to launch such a service, such as the need for a mobile lab to do quick tests (ScanRDI Lite?) and knowledge transfer sessions. In the foreseeable future, some firm will launch this service because the good compounding pharmacies will want to exceed the FDA and state regulatory agency guidelines while providing life-saving and life-enhancing drugs to patients. PCCA is well poised to lead the industry in providing this service.

SUMMARY

Pharmacy compounding in the supply chain world is a bridge between Titles I and II of the Drug Quality and Security Act. There are three main parts to this supply chain: from doctor prescription/patient demand to ingredients, from ingredients to compounding pharmacies, and from compounding pharmacies to patients in need of the compounded medicines.

We reviewed PCCA in depth, covering order aggregation and supplier sourcing, order placement to PCCA receipt of bulk ingredients, and compounding pharmacy order-fill processes. We reviewed the compounding pharmacies to patients part of the supply chain, and at a very high level discussed clean rooms for sterile compounding of drugs.

We also reviewed current good manufacturing practices in some depth. Additionally, we proposed for the compounding pharmacies to seek out an accredited independent audit firm (i.e., AIB International) to do self-audits at the highest standard of both FDA audits and state board of pharmacy audits. We briefly discussed good laboratory practices and good clinical practices. We ended the chapter with a review of Eagle Analytical Services and their support of compounding pharmacies. These services utilize state-of-the-art technology and range from testing samples and formulas to providing feedback techniques to pharmacists at compounding pharmacies.

It only takes one New England Compounding Center and a lack of current good manufacturing practices and good laboratory practices to produce real and present danger to patient safety. The compounding pharmacy supply chain by and large appears to have safe controls and good practices up to the compounding pharmacies themselves. The upcoming audit requirements will (hopefully) be structured to ensure patient safety through solid controls and adherence to good practices. It is up to the compounding pharmacies to step forward and be on the offensive in terms of subscribing to external audits. Otherwise, these pharmacies will always be on the defensive in terms of audit compliance and at risk for catastrophic mistakes.

ENDNOTES

1. PCCA permission.
2. Ilisa B.G. Bernstein, Getting Ready for the Drug Supply Chain Security Act (Title II of the Drug Quality and Security Act), presented at Association of Food and Drug Officials Education Conference, June 13, 2014.
3. What Are Compounding Pharmacies, WebMD, http://www.webmd.com/brain/news/20121010/what-are-compounding-pharmacies.
4. Jeffrey W. Koehler, conversations during his studies at Tulane.
5. Sterile Environment, Biology Online, http://www.biology-online.org/dictionary/Sterile_-_Environment.
6. J.D. Willey, as told to Fred Kuglin in Houston, TX, July 11, 2014.
7. Melinda Wenner, Humans Carry More Bacterial Cells than Human Ones, *Scientific American*, 2007, http://www.scientificamerican.com/article/strange-but-true-humans-carry-more-bacterial-cells-than-human-ones/.
8. Current Good Manufacturing Practices (CGMPs)/Compliance, FDA, http://www.fda.gov/drugs/guidancecomplianceregulatoryinformation/guidances/ucm064971.htm.
9. FDA, Silver Spring, MD, conversations with FDA representatives on June 16 and June 23, 2014.
10. AIB International, http://www.aibonline.org/aibOnline/en/.
11. Glossary, Project on Government Oversight, http://www.pogo.org/investigations/glossary.html.
12. 21 CFR 58—Good Laboratory Practice Regulations, p. 1, Section 5.8.3, Definitions, http://www.21cfrpart11.com/files/library/pred_rules/mcdowall_glp_annotate.pdf.
13. Glossary, Duke Clinical Research Institute, https://www.dcri.org/trial-participation/glossary.
14. Company Profile, Eagle Analytical Services, https://www.eagleanalytical.com/sitecontent/576/company-profile/category/459/about-eagle.aspx.
15. William J. Zolner, The ScanRDI Sterility Test Protocol as an Effective and Reliable Test for Sterile Compounded Preparations, Eagle Analytical Services White Paper, Houston, TX, pp. 1–2.
16. Ibid., pp. 6–7.

4

Track and Trace: Not Hide and Seek

OVERVIEW

In the first three chapters, we focused on Title I: Compounding Quality Act of the Drug Quality and Security Act. In this chapter, we review Title II: Drug Supply Chain Security Act (sometimes called the track and trace part of the law). Efforts are underway to plan the necessary steps to build an electronic system to identify and trace prescription drugs as they are distributed in the United States. As I was writing this book, the targeted completion for this system was November 27, 2024, or 10 years from the signing of the H.R. 3204 bill into law and the enactment of the Drug Quality and Security Act.

It is planned (hoped?) that this system will allow for the exchange of information "at the package level" about where a drug has been in the supply chain. There are three objectives for this new system:

1. Enable verification of the legitimacy of the drug product identifier down to the package level
2. Enhance detection and notification of illegitimate products in the drug supply chain
3. Facilitate more efficient recalls of drug products[1]

During a conversation with the Food and Drug Administration (FDA), it was explained to me that the FDA is relying on the manufacturers, wholesale distributors, repackagers, and large pharmacy chains to work with them to develop this system over the next decade. Several Big Data information technology providers and consulting firms have also expressed interest in participating to develop this system.

KEY PROVISIONS

The FDA has identified the key provisions (and their requirements) to be implemented over the next 10 years:

- Product identification
- Product tracing
- Product verification
- Detection and response
- Notification
- Wholesale licensing
- Third-party logistics provider licensing[2]

This is a huge undertaking by the FDA and the industry as a whole. Let's take a look at each provision in depth.

Product Identification

The FDA is requiring manufacturers and repackagers to put a unique product identifier on certain prescription drug packages. An example of this unique product identifier is the use of a barcode that can be easily read electronically.[3] Traditional linear barcodes are used today, but are limited in their data storage capacity (Figure 4.1).

So what are certain prescription drug packages? Why are some pharmaceutical drugs exempt, while others are not? Regarding the barcode, the current FDA regulations require that certain human drug and biological

ABC-abc-1234

FIGURE 4.1
Linear barcode. (From Online Barcode Generator, TEC-IT, http://barcode.tec-it.com/barcode-generator.aspx. With permission.)

FIGURE 4.2
Two-dimensional barcode. (From Online Barcode Generator, TEC-IT, http://barcode.
tec-it.com/barcode-generator.aspx. With permission.)

product labels contain at a minimum the National Drug Code (NDC) number (21 CFR 201.25).[4] Not surprisingly, the FDA chose 2D barcodes over the use of radio frequency identification (RFID) tags (Figure 4.2). I was told by an anonymous FDA representative that to store the amount of data required, an active RFID tag would have to be used. Active RFID tags cost $15 to $100 each. Misreads can also be an issue when the battery-powered active RFID tags lose power.[5]

Product Tracing

The FDA is requiring manufacturers, wholesale distributors, repackagers, and pharmacies in the drug supply chain to provide information about a drug and who handled it each time it is sold in the U.S. market.[6] So the information about a drug should be defined as the primary suppliers of compounds, fine chemicals, and inert ingredients. This implies that suppliers such as the Professional Compounding Centers of America (PCCA) must initiate the pedigree so that its pharmacies can comply with this requirement. Paper pedigrees already exist for certain drugs, as PCCA is doing to meet the Florida pedigree law standards. Will the new requirements be different, or more of the same?

What is yet to be determined is whether the information about a drug includes the sources of packaging material. This is extremely important, as it relates to tamper-resistant and tamper-evident packaging. In addition, the "who handled it each time it is sold" requirement misses a key point. A pharmaceutical drug product can be handled by a wholesale distributor and a transportation carrier without selling the drug product. Whether the drug product is sold "FOB Origin" or "FOB Destination," there may be a physical change in handing of the drug product without change in ownership. (FOB means freight on board, or in layperson's terms, who pays the freight.) If the purpose is to trace a product to prevent product substitution or product adulteration, the wording of this requirement leaves out a key item. Also, if the FDA changes its mind and requires compounded drugs to be tracked, how does someone trace a product that is converted from a powder to a liquid?

Product Verification

The FDA is requiring manufacturers, wholesale distributors, repackagers, and many dispensers (primarily pharmacies) to establish systems and processes to be able to verify the product identifier on certain prescription drug packages.[7] There are two issues with how this one is worded by the FDA. The first issue is the use of the word *identifier*. Currently there are companies that provide multiple layers of identifiers on the drug packages, from overt to covert to forensic markers. The bad guys are smart—one singular identifier? It won't take long for the bad guys to figure it out. The second issue revolves around the question of who will verify the product identifier. I feel that the FDA is behind the curve on what is happening in the marketplace on product verification.

Detection and Response

The FDA is requiring manufacturers, wholesale distributors, repackagers, and many dispensers (primarily pharmacies) to quarantine and promptly investigate a drug that has been identified as suspect, meaning that it may be counterfeit, unapproved, or potentially dangerous.[8] This is a very good requirement, and most of the good companies already do the proper investigation. The investigation is only as strong as the weakest link in the supply chain. Education, training, and common processes and procedures are needed across all entities. In addition, every company will need a strong internal audit/security group to deal with issues when they arise.

Notification

The FDA is requiring manufacturers, wholesale distributors, repackagers, and many dispensers (primarily pharmacies) to establish systems and processes to notify the FDA and other stakeholders if an illegitimate drug is found.[9] The internal audit/security groups will need to know not only how and to whom they need to report the finding of an illegitimate drug, but also, more importantly, when to pass along their investigations to governing agencies and law enforcement for their handling.

Wholesale Distributor Licensing

The FDA is requiring wholesale distributors to report their licensing status and contact information to the FDA. This information will then be made available in a public database.[10] Perhaps the sheer size of some of the wholesale distributors is driving this need on the contact information.

Third-Party Logistics Provider Licensing

The FDA is requiring that third-party logistic providers, those who provide storage and logistical operations related to drug distribution, obtain a state or federal license.[11] This is actually a very good and long overdue requirement. During the first year, ending November 27, 2014, third-party logistics providers reported to the secretary of Health and Human Services the state by which their facilities are licensed, the appropriate identification number of such license, and the name and address of the facilities and all trade names under which such facilities conduct business. By 2017, there are a series of regulations to be developed to govern the activities of third-party logistics providers to bring them into the fold of the pharmaceutical drug supply chain.[12]

The upcoming regulations will include the licensing process based on a to-be-developed accreditation program; drug-safe and secure storage practices, including a quarantine area for facilities; and written policies and procedures that address the receipt, security, storage, inventory, shipment, and distribution of a product. These policies and procedures shall also include the identity, record, and report of confirmed losses or thefts in the United States; correct errors and inaccuracies in inventories; provide support for manufacturer recalls; prepare for, protect against, and address any reasonably foreseeable crisis that affects security or operation at the facility, such as a strike, fire, or flood; and ensure that any expired product is segregated from other products and returned to the manufacturer or repackager or destroyed. These policies and procedures shall also maintain the capability to trace the receipt and outbound distribution of a product, and supplies and records of inventory, and quarantine or destroy a suspect product if directed to do so by the respective manufacturer, wholesale distributor, dispenser, or an authorized government agency. (This appears to be directed at return logistics providers, which we will cover in Chapter 7.) These regulations also provide for periodic inspections by the licensing authority and background checks for personnel with strict regulations on the hiring of known felons in specific, related categories.[13]

FROM PLANNING TO EXECUTION

The FDA is working hard to comply with the Drug Quality and Security Act's requirements. There are a lot of questions to be answered, followed by policies and procedures to be implemented for all participants in the pharmaceutical drug supply chain. The development of standards and pilot programs with the industry supply chain participants places the FDA in an unenviable position of getting a consensus among disparate interests. Protecting consumers from counterfeit, adulterated, and contaminated drugs that can be harmful is a very good objective.

Protecting industry participants from stolen drugs is also a very good objective. As I identified in the introduction, prescription painkillers are very popular with the drug cartels. According to a survey, the cost to buy prescription painkillers at a pharmacy versus the street corner is about the same.[14] How do the bad guys get the prescription painkillers to sell through the illegal market at the same price as the local pharmacy? The simple answer is that they must be stealing the drugs. The FDA is trying to put together a program to address the weaknesses in the pharmaceutical drug supply chain.

Some observers have been asking the question, "Didn't we try this before with ePedigree?" The answer is in part yes and in part no. Let's take a look at the ePedigree initiative, why it did not take hold as a program, and what can be done differently with the Drug Quality and Security Act.

BACK TO THE FUTURE

The FDA defines a drug pedigree as a statement of origin that identifies each prior sale, purchase, or trade of a drug, including the date of those transactions and the names and addresses of all parties to them.[15] An electronic pedigree, or ePedigree, is an electronic pedigree document.

In early 2007, EPCglobal ratified the pedigree standard as an international standard that specified an Extensive Markup Language (XML) description of the life history of a drug product. The basic data elements of an original ePedigree were defined as lot, potency, national drug code and electronic drug code, manufacturer, wholesale distributor, pharmacy, and unique identifier of the saleable unit.[16]

California took the lead in defining the saleable unit as a pill and requiring the tracking and tracing of drug products down to the pill level. Hopes were high to have a nationwide program to track and trace drugs through the supply chain. States rushed in to pass ePedigree laws of their own, and in a short 18 months we had (and still have) a spiderweb of ePedigree laws. Today, in many states ePedigree amounts to putting paper pedigrees into a Word, Excel spreadsheet, or PDF format. What happened?

In 2007–2008 I was personally involved with ePedigree, working as a supply chain consultant to a couple of participants in an ePedigree solution. In my opinion, there are a few reasons why ePedigree was doomed to fail to live up to its hype.

There was no national law that dictated how the data would be interchanged between supply chain participants and who controlled those data. What happened is that the data interchange was dummied down to the simplest electronic form, losing most of the value of the data in the process. There were enormous privacy issues regarding who controlled the data that could not be addressed at the time. In addition, the myriad state requirements made the sharing of data challenging, at best.

There was no single point of contact to figure out how to protect the data, given the many formats and entry points. Some of the "big iron" companies (manufacturers of mainframes, servers, and data storage machines) approached the problem in a centralized manner. This did not work for a distributed supply chain, and the challenge to handle the massive amount of data was immense, to say the least. In many respects, this became a data storage and data management program, not a pharmaceutical drug track and trace security program.

The push was to track pharmaceutical drugs down to the pill level. What happens when pills from multiple lots are put into dispensers at local pharmacies? What happens to pills that become liquefied during pharmacy compounding? I have no idea how this idealistic objective actually took hold as a real-world objective.

Of course, there was the 600-pound gorilla sitting in the room. The big question on everyone's mind was, who is going to pay for all of this? The global financial crisis put a big damper on the ePedigree movement beyond putting paper pedigrees in simple electronic format, and in many respects it was shelved as a coordinated national and global program.

THE SILVER LINING: SERIALIZATION

Throughout the ePedigree process, what was evident was that the technology was beginning to be in place to make track and trace a reality. Today, electronic track and trace can be done with existing technology and meet the upcoming product identification and product tracing regulations. The challenge comes with transferring the transaction data between entities in the supply chain. Each entity is likely to have its own technical standards and data definitions, and, in order to safeguard its information technology infrastructure, may not be willing to collaborate with other entities to deploy an efficient solution. By 2015, this change needs to be made manually, and by November 27, 2017, this change must be made electronically. The product identifier on all drug products must be imprinted or affixed on the label at the product and the case level.

The companies that have been working toward the California ePedigree standards may have a jump-start on the new track and trace mandate. One company example that falls into this category is Pfizer. "At Pfizer, we've been preparing for the California mandate for several years, so we are able to leverage that work to prepare for the federal mandate," says Peggy Staver, Director, Product Integrity. "The Pfizer team is continuing to deploy serialization throughout Pfizer packaging lines and is building out a cloud-based IT solution that integrates with the company's contract manufacturers to ensure Pfizer meets the November 2017 compliance deadline for lot-level serialization."[17]

In addition, serialization laws have been in place in other countries. Michael Lewis, president and founder at Frequentz, a track and trace technology specialist, says, "The U.S. serialization law lags behind those of other countries. This law has marginal to no impact on the overall global traceability requirements and planning efforts. Serialization laws and regulations have already been piloted, if not fully executed abroad."[18] The companies that are struggling with the new track and trace regulations are the ones that have deferred action in the past regarding serialization.

There exist a number of challenges in achieving true serialization in the pharma supply chain. Serialization is more than a simple print and apply process of a label to a product. The challenge with serialization is storing the various pieces of information associated with the unique identifier that will be the drug's lot-level serial number. Each time the product moves in the supply chain or product ownership transfers, the pertinent chain of custody information must be captured. This increases the complexity of both the capture and storage requirements exponentially as the product moves in the supply chain farther and farther toward the ultimate consumer, the patient.

There are a number of serialization companies domestically and internationally that provide the product identifier on the label or "license plate" for the drug product and cases. For simple products, current barcode labels will suffice. For more complex drug products, the 2D barcode with its greater storage capacity will be needed. The challenge will be for these providers to readjust their equipment to meet the upcoming regulations. However, to do a pilot, the serialization technology to affix the product identifier is already in existence.

THE SILVER LINING: TRACK AND TRACE TECHNOLOGY

A good analogy for serialization is that all cars, trucks, and motorcycles on the roadways are now required to have license plates. All packaged drugs now have or will have a serialized label. This is a solid start. What is the next step?

It is absolutely critical to have a track and trace system that will be able to receive input data from the serialized labels on pharmaceutical drug packages, track the pharmaceutical drugs through the supply chain, and trace these same drugs back through the supply chain when issues arise. This is no easy task!

There are several companies that claim they have the supply chain track and trace solution to meet the requirements (or yet to be determined requirements) for the Drug Quality and Security Act. IBM and SAP are marketing their solutions to pharmaceutical supply chain participants. Bosch Packaging Technology is also marketing its solutions, with a stronger focus on its serialization capabilities.[19]

Tracelink offers a cloud-based solution that, through its network management services, allows the entire supply chain participants to connect with one another. It offers product tracing, product and transaction verification, product serialization, and compliance data archival services through modular, off-the-shelf applications. Tracelink's solution reaches out and identifies inventory levels in the supply chain to improve forecasting. What I really like is its capability to provide supply chain participants with government reporting solutions through its modular applications.[20]

Another track and trace technology provider is One Network Enterprises. One Network was founded by Greg Brady in 2002. One Network provides its global pharmaceutical drug fulfillment service to the marketplace, which uses real-time supply information to meet actual demand. The result is an optimization of the distribution of pharmaceutical drugs and other critical medical supplies and equipment to clinics, hospitals, pharmacies, and patients around the globe.[21]

One Network also uses a cloud platform, which enables all supply chain participants to manage and track demand on a permissions-based basis. One Network's service is input agnostic, so it does not matter whether labels, 2D barcodes, or RFID tags are used for serialization. Once the input templates are initially established, the inputs are recognized and used by its service. Using real-time supply and supply chain conditions, the One Network service manages replenishment, inventory and order management, chain of custody, lot and expiration management, and other logistics processes in real time.[22]

What I personally like about One Network is the ability to match demand with supply in a real-time manner. The result is an acceleration of inventory and working capital turns while minimizing stock-outs. From a patient safety standpoint, this is extremely important. What I also like about One Network is its ability to "nest" and track products. One Network can track pills into blister packs, blister packs into caddies, caddies into cases, cases onto pallets, and all of the above to production lot numbers. This is impressive, and exactly what the FDA is trying to require with its track and trace requirements![23]

Tracelink and One Network are two providers that can pull together serialization and track and trace for solutions to the FDA track and trace requirements. There are other providers in the marketplace, but I feel these two providers have differentiated themselves with their services.

THE SILVER LINING: THE AUTHENTICATION CONNECTION

During my many conversations with supply chain professionals and FDA representatives regarding the track and trace requirements, the subject of

```
┌─────────────────────────────────────────────────────────────┐
│  Example of a Serialized National Drug Code (sNDC)            │
│                                                               │
│        NDC                      SERIAL NUMBER                 │
│                                                               │
│     55555 666 77      +     11111111111111111111              │
│                                                               │
│  Labeler code + product code unique, up to 20 characters + package code │
└─────────────────────────────────────────────────────────────┘
```

FIGURE 4.3
An sNDC example. (From Guidance for Industry: Standards for Securing the Drug Supply Chain—Standardized Numerical Identification for Prescription Drug Packages, U.S. Food and Drug Administration, 2010, p. 7, http://www.fda.gov/downloads/RegulatoryInformation/Guidances/UCM206075.pdf.)

authentication always surfaces. However, in many to most cases, the definition of *authentication* is skewed toward authentication of the packaging. The logic seems to be, if you can authenticate the packaging, you can authenticate the pharmaceutical drugs in the packaging.

In March 2010, the FDA issued its *Guidance for Industry Standards for Securing the Drug Supply Chain—Standardized Numerical Identification for Prescription Drug Packages.*[24] This guidance calls for the development of a standard numerical identification (SNI) to be applied to the smallest package for individual sale in a pharmacy. The basis for the SNI is a serialized National Drug Code (sNDC) (see Figure 4.3).

As we mentioned at the start of this chapter, the supply chain participants are now being asked to establish the processes and systems to verify the product identifier (or SNI). Of course, this is a good start to secure the pharmaceutical drug supply chain. However, verifying the product identifier only verifies the "license plate." In my opinion, this is *not* product authentication. I have always defined *product authentication* as confirming truth or integrity of the pharmaceutical drug. When all is said and done, the people responsible for patient safety and the patients want the drug product authenticated. Verifying the product identifier is only one step to product authentication.

ENTER THE BAD GUYS—AND GALS

The FDA asking the supply chain participants to establish the process and systems to verify the product identifier potentially leaves the door wide open for the bad guys and gals to figure out how to beat the system. If the process and systems that are developed get too granular, they are at risk for substitution and circumvention.

There are no foolproof processes or systems. There are, however, complexities within processes and systems that can deter the amateurs and not-so-sophisticated counterfeiters, diverters, and thieves. The objective is to provide safe, affordable drugs to patients while protecting the revenue stream for the brand or pharmaceutical drug owners. A secondary objective is to catch the bad guys and gals and put them out of business.

AUTHENTIX

There are many nanotech companies in the marketplace. One company—Authentix, Inc.—stands out in its ability to combine innovative nanoscale covert marking technology, industry-leading authentication expertise, and proven program management experience for its clients.

Authentix provides comprehensive authentication solutions for pharmaceutical, over-the-counter, and nutrition products as well as their packaging, and can help in tracking their source or intended use in distribution. Authentix takes a beginning-to-end approach, and provides fully integrated programs that enable manufacturers and pharmaceutical supply chain participants to protect their products in the ever-complex supply and distribution chains. Authentix helps its customers achieve results by placing nanoscale covert markers in the product and on multiple levels of the packaging. When fully implemented, this approach allows manufacturers to authenticate the display packaging, dispensing packaging, individual units, and the product itself as it moves through the supply chain from manufacture through retail and into returns and warranty.

These solutions are complementary to serialization technologies to enhance the manufacturer's ability to track and trace its products through the supply chain. In addition, through partner-provided fieldwork, Authentix is able to detect where, when, and how diversion or substitution of product occurs. By virtue of their work, Authentix solutions are used by many of the top pharmaceutical and life science companies in the United States and Europe.

As we mentioned, Authentix focuses on using multiple covert marking strategies to authenticate pharmaceutical drug products and their packaging to prevent counterfeiting and diversion. This way, the bad guys and gals can crack the code on one or two of the markers, thinking they have circumvented the authentication process—leaving them open to being caught in the process.

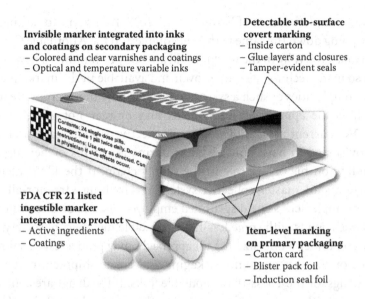

Invisible marker integrated into inks and coatings on secondary packaging
– Colored and clear varnishes and coatings
– Optical and temperature variable inks

Detectable sub-surface covert marking
– Inside carton
– Glue layers and closures
– Tamper-evident seals

FDA CFR 21 listed ingestible marker integrated into product
– Active ingredients
– Coatings

Item-level marking on primary packaging
– Carton card
– Blister pack foil
– Induction seal foil

FIGURE 4.4
Authentix: Packaging and product layering of markers. (From Authentix. With permission.)

The layered approach takes advantage of multiple marker and detector technologies to provide the right usability and total program cost to match the regulatory risk and brand protection profile of the manufacturer. Authentix provides invisible markers that can be integrated into printed inks and coatings that can be detected using a simple and small handheld reader. Forensic-level protections can be provided with molecular markers that are tested in a laboratory setting using instruments common to evidence used in court cases. And in-product marking is done using recognition markers that can be tested in the field or in a laboratory to show authenticity. Combined, these markers help protect the pharmaceutical drug products, their packaging, and the safety of patients like you and me. They also protect the drug brand and its associated revenues through the avoidance of counterfeiting, substitution, or diversion (Figure 4.4).[25]

EPEDIGREE: ACT 2?

At the beginning of this chapter, I stated that it is the FDA's guideline to "plan the necessary steps to build an electronic system to identify and trace prescription drugs as they are distributed in the United States," with a targeted completion date of November 27, 2023. Excuse me for asking, but are we going down the same path as ePedigree and the Affordable Care Act or Obamacare? Why in the world would anybody be building a new system when so many technologies are proven and available in the marketplace?

The complexities of such a system to provide only the appropriate information to the appropriate individuals may or may not go far beyond the FDA's current capabilities. With a collective system, each user must be provisioned to have only certain information at his or her disposal, depending on his or her role in the supply chain. If the FDA intends a one-size-fits-all, master-collective system, it is inviting a free-for-all.

For example, let's say a disgruntled employee of a major distributor has just made friends with some less-than-reputable members of society. This employee, under a one-size-fits-all approach, may grab a few serial numbers he or she sees on some packaging and create shipment patterns of some drugs for these less-than-reputable folks. If the drugs are controlled substances with a convertible street value, they may only be at risk of being stolen from the supply chain. What if the less-than-reputable individual has plans to resell the product back into legitimate channels?

Remember, if the product is particularly temperature sensitive or has specialized handling guidelines, the criminals aren't playing by the rules. They won't care about whom they hurt, since they are already playing outside of the rules. It then only takes a shady pharmacy looking to boost its profits to fabricate the pedigree in the system and pay less than market rates. Sure, it might be discoverable, but with the sheer size of all the data the FDA is likely to encounter, will it find out in time? At risk in this potential free-for-all are the ultimate consumers—patients.

WHERE DO WE GO FROM HERE?

We live in a world of distributed computing and cloud computing. The sharing of technology infrastructures on a secure, permissions-based basis would allow for people within a pharmaceutical drug supply chain network to track and trace pharmaceutical drugs in a cost-efficient manner. It would also allow the private marketplace to leverage existing capabilities and not have to bear the expense of migrating to a new centralized system.

My suggestion is to develop two side-by-side feasibility studies. One study would use 2D barcodes and the other would use RFID tags. These studies would be anchored by major pharmaceutical drug companies and incorporate specific wholesale distributors, pharmaceutical retailers, and return logistics providers. The feasibility studies would embrace specific serialization, authentication, and supply chain track and trace network providers, and would be carried out under the guidance of the FDA. Due to the cost of the active RFID tags, perhaps the pilot using them would only focus on high-value, time-sensitive pharmaceutical drug products.

The technologies are available to put these two pilots or feasibility studies into practice in 6 to 9 months. Real-world feasibility studies would allow the two sets of teams to plan and implement the tracking and tracing of pharmaceutical drugs, test the results, and replan and reimplement with the appropriate modifications. The private sector can blow by the objectives of the FDA in 10 years to provide product and transaction information at each point of sale with lot information and place unique product identifiers on individual packages. With two distinct feasibility studies and with distributed and cloud computing, both approaches may be acceptable within the FDA guidelines without a massive conversion to a centralized government system.

Once again, the question will surface, who is going to pay for all of this? In the long run, two pilots or feasibility studies with existing capabilities and executed by the private sector will be vastly less expensive than a new engineered system built by the federal government to encompass any and all conditions and situations. It will also compress the time between planning and implementation, saving lives of patients as well as enormous amounts of money.

Also, having two pilots or feasibility studies will foster competition and cooperation if properly guided by the FDA. The real winners will be the FDA and, more importantly, the general public.

SUMMARY

We started the chapter by identifying that the Title II: Drug Supply Chain Security Act has three objectives: (1) enable verification of the legitimacy of the drug product identifier down to the package level, (2) enhance detection and notification of illegitimate products in the drug supply chain, and (3) facilitate more efficient recalls of drug products. We proceeded to review the seven key provisions of Title II, and to compare the past ePedigree initiative with Title II. We also cited examples of Authentix, Tracelink, and One Network as having capabilities to meet or exceed FDA requirements in Title II regarding authentication, tracking, and tracing of pharmaceutical drugs. The direction is positive, but many pitfalls remain for the pharmaceutical drug supply chain participants as the FDA defines the final regulations under Title II.

ENDNOTES

1. Drug Supply Chain Security Act (DSCSA), FDA, http://www.fda.gov/Drugs/Drug-Safety/DrugIntegrityandSupplyChainSecurity/DrugSupplyChainSecurityAct/.
2. Ibid.
3. Ibid.
4. CFR—Code of Federal Regulations Title 21, FDA, http://www.accessdata.fda.gov/scripts/cdrh/cfdocs/cfcfr/CFRSearch.cfm?fr=201.25.
5. Active RFID vs. Passive RFID, Atlas RFID Solutions, http://atlasrfid.com/auto-id-education/active-vs-passive-rfid/.
6. Drug Supply Chain Security Act (DSCSA), FDA, http://www.fda.gov/Drugs/Drug-Safety/DrugIntegrityandSupplyChainSecurity/DrugSupplyChainSecurityAct/.
7. Ibid.
8. Ibid.
9. Ibid.
10. Ibid.
11. Ibid.
12. 21 U.S. Code § 360eee—3, Legal Information Institute, http://www.law.cornell.edu/uscode/text/21/360eee-3.
13. Ibid.
14. Tyler Durden, Top 10 Facts about the U.S. Illegal Drug Market, Zero Hedge, 2013, http://www.zerohedge.com/news/2013-10-30/top-10-facts-about-us-illegal-drug-market.
15. Guidance for Industry, FDA, http://www.fda.gov/downloads/Drugs/Guidance-ComplianceRegulatoryInformation/Guidances/UCM134399.pdf.
16. http://en.wikipedia.org/wiki/Epedigree.
17. Gail Dutton, Serialization—Pharma Faces 2015 Deadline, Pharmaceutical Online, 2014, http://www.pharmaceuticalonline.com/doc/serialization-pharma-faces-deadline-0001.
18. Ibid.
19. Trace and Track, Bosch Packaging Technology, http://www.boschpackaging.com/en/pa/services/after-sales-services/modernization/track-and-trace/track-and-trace-4.html.
20. http://tracelink.com/inventory-demand-forecast-visibility-solutions.
21. One Network Launches New Global Fulfillment Service for Medicine, One Network Enterprises, http://www.onenetwork.com/2013/09/one-network-launches-new-global-fulfillment-service-medicine/.
22. Personal observations with past demos of the One Network solution.

23. One Network Launches New Global Fulfillment Service for Medicine, One Network Enterprises, http://www.onenetwork.com/2013/09/one-network-launches-new-global-fulfillment-service-medicine/.
24. Guidance for Industry, FDA, http://www.fda.gov/downloads/RegulatoryInformation/Guidances/UCM206075.pdf.
25. http://www.authentix.com/; Ryon Packer, Chief Marketing Officer and General Manager, Brand Division, Authentix, Inc., September 18, 2014.

5

Land of the Giants— and Land of the Totes

OVERVIEW

Virtually all of us have gone through the process of getting a prescription filled at a local pharmacy. There are certain rituals that must go on to get our needed pharmaceutical drugs. First, except for over-the-counter drugs, we need a prescription approved or signed by a licensed physician or doctor. This prescription will be sent to the pharmacy electronically or called in by the physician's office (more than likely a nurse on behalf of a doctor). Sometimes a paper copy of the prescription is given to the patient in order to be given to the pharmacist.

Next, we stand in line for a long time with the rest of the sick people, waiting on our prescription. This is a little humor because we are usually not feeling well, and any wait for our needed pharmaceutical drugs can seem like an eternity. However, have we ever thought how the drugs prescribed by our doctors get to the local pharmacy? The average pharmacy ranges from 800 to 2,000 square feet to handle 5,000 to 8,000 stock-keeping units and fill 200 to 400 prescriptions a day, with high-volume pharmacies filling up to 600 prescriptions per day.[1] Yet there have been 1,453 drugs that have obtained Food and Drug Administration (FDA) approval as of December 31, 2013, with over 100,000 stock-keeping units available for patients.[2] How does the math work so we get our prescriptions filled when we need them? The answer is a combination of wholesale distributors and company-owned forward distribution centers.

THE BIG THREE

It is estimated that 85% of all pharmaceutical drug distribution revenues are generated by three companies: McKesson Corporation, Cardinal Health, Inc., and AmerisourceBergen Corporation.[3] There are two types of wholesale distributors in the pharmaceutical drug industry: full-line wholesale distributors and specialty wholesale distributors. Full-line wholesale distributors contract with major pharmaceutical drug manufacturers to buy, inventory, and sell their full pharmaceutical product lines. Specialty distributors contract with pharmaceutical drug manufacturers to buy, inventory, and sell specialty pharmaceutical drugs primarily to hospitals, physician-owned/operated clinics, and hospital-owned outpatient clinics.[4] Oncology products account for almost half of sales by specialty distributors.[5]

The revenues by the big three tell part of the story. For fiscal year 2014, McKesson Corporation was the largest wholesale distributor, with $137.609 billion in revenues, followed by AmerisourceBergen, with $118.45 billion in revenues, and Cardinal Health, with $90.07 billion in revenues (Figure 5.1).[6]

The big three are also the largest specialty wholesale distributors. AmerisourceBergen Specialty Group (ABSG) has Oncology Supply, ASD Healthcare, and Besse Medical; McKesson has McKesson Specialty; and Cardinal Health has its Special Pharmacy Distribution and Special Pharmacy Solutions.[7] How did the big three become the big three? Let's take a look at the history of each of these large companies.

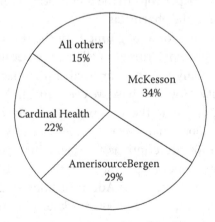

FIGURE 5.1

Fiscal year 2014 revenues. (From Fred A. Kuglin, with data from Charles Schwab Stock Research Summary, July 2014.)

MCKESSON COMPANY: THE LARGEST AND THE OLDEST*

McKesson Corporation is both the largest wholesale distributor in the United States and the oldest. Its history dates back 181 years, when John McKesson and Charles Olcott founded McKesson in 1833 in New York City. The company was founded to import and sell therapeutic drugs and chemicals. It quickly started stocking the medicine chests aboard trade ships with pharmaceutical drugs imported from Europe, and started selling medicinal herbs, roots, and spices from Pennsylvania Shaker colonies. In 1853, the company was renamed McKesson & Robbins. By then, the company was distributing pharmaceutical products by covered wagon to 17 states and territories across America, from Vermont to California.[8]

In 1855, McKesson & Robbins became one of the first wholesale firms to manufacture drugs. In the early 1900s, McKesson & Robbins persuaded several well-established wholesalers to become its subsidiaries, forming a national drug wholesaling company and becoming the leading distributor of pharmaceutical drug products in the United States (Figure 5.2).

FIGURE 5.2
McKesson & Robbins headquarters, post-1853. (From McKesson. With permission.)

---

* The following is a summary of the history of McKesson Corporation from its website.

During the 1960s, McKesson & Robbins continued its focus on distribution by merging with Foremost Dairies of San Francisco to form Foremost-McKesson, Inc. The new company became the largest U.S. distributor of pharmaceutical drugs, alcoholic beverages, and chemicals; the largest supplier of whey by-products; the largest producer of processed water; a leader in the fresh dairy products field; and a multiregional distributor of hospital and laboratory supplies and equipment.

In the 1980s and 1990s, McKesson decided to focus more on health care and divested its unrelated businesses. The company acquired Automated Health Care, now part of McKesson Automation, and General Medical, the largest distributor of medical-surgical supplies. The company also acquired HBO & Company and operated for a time as McKesson HBOC—the world's largest health care services company.[9]

Today, McKesson is ranked 15th on the Fortune 500, with more than $137.6 billion in annual revenue. The company delivers pharmaceutical drugs, medical supplies, and health care information technology solutions through a network of 29 distribution centers, a primary distribution center, a strategic redistribution center, and two repackaging facilities.[10]

AMERISOURCEBERGEN[*]

Lucien Napoleon Brunswig is credited with being the founder of Bergen Brunswig. He was born in 1854 and immigrated to the United States in approximately 1871. He became an apprentice to a U.S. druggist at 17 years old, and opened his own drug store in Atchison, Kansas, when he was 21. He sold the Kansas store, opened a new store in Ft. Worth, and by 1882 was invited by George R. Finlay to join him as a partner in a drug wholesale business. The new firm was called Finlay Brunswig until 1885 and Finlay's death. In 1887 Brunswig took on a partner, F.W. Braun. They opened operations out west, and in 1907, Brunswig bought out Braun. The new business was renamed Brunswig Drug Company. Brunswig died in 1943, two years after his retirement; he did not live to see his kingdom expand tremendously, as it did in the years following World War II.[11]

In 1947 Emil P. Martini founded and became the first president of the Bergen Drug Company based in Hackensack, New Jersey. A

---

[*] The following is a summary of the history of AmerisourceBergen from fundinguniverse.com/companies-history and AmerisourceBergen's website.

well-established member of the community and president of the New Jersey State Board of Pharmacy, Martini helped establish a wholesale drug distribution company in 1947 named after the county of Bergen, in which they lived. The success of the Bergen Drug Company was phenomenal, in part because of the insatiable demand for the wonder drugs of World War II, including such antibiotics as penicillin. Despite the growing sales volume, the company continued to offer same-day service.

With the 1955 death of Emil P. Martini Sr., leadership of the company was turned over to Martini's son, Emil P. Martini Jr. The Bergen Drug Company then began rapidly expanding and acquiring other wholesale drug companies. In May 1969, Martini successfully negotiated the purchase of Brunswig Drug Corporation. The name of the new company was the Bergen Brunswig Corporation. Bergen Brunswig became an innovator in electronic data interchange (EDI) transmissions of purchase orders, handheld computer scanners, automated distribution centers, and next-day delivery to pharmacies.[12]

Alco Standard Corporation purchased The Drug House in 1977, and in 1985 became known as Alco Health Services Corporation. AHSC Holdings Corporation acquired Alco Health Services Corporation in 1988 through a management-led buyout, and in 1994 changed its name to AmeriSource Health Corporation. Two large acquisitions were made in 1999: C.D. Smith Healthcare and a substantial share of ADDS Telepharmacy Solutions, Inc.[13]

In 2001, AmeriSource Health Corporation merged with Bergen Brunswig Corporation to form AmerisourceBergen Corporation. Today, Amerisource-Bergen is a leader in global pharmaceutical sourcing and distribution services and has the largest global generics purchasing organization. AmerisourceBergen has 26 U.S. pharmaceutical distribution centers, 4 U.S. specialty distribution centers, and 2 Canadian distribution centers in North America.[14]

CARDINAL HEALTH[*]

Cardinal Health is a relative newcomer to the big three vis-à-vis McKesson and AmerisourceBergen. Cardinal Health was founded in 1971 by Robert D. Walter when he opened a small distribution center

---

[*] The following is a summary of the history of Cardinal Health from the Cardinal Health website.

in Columbus, Ohio. In less than a decade, the then-named Cardinal Foods became a prominent regional food distributor until branching into pharmaceutical distribution in 1979. That was the year the company purchased a Zanesville, Ohio, drug distributor and became known as Cardinal Distribution.[15]

In 1983, Cardinal Health went public. In 1988, Cardinal Health sold its food distribution segment to focus on its pharmaceutical distribution business. Cardinal Health achieved $1 billion in revenue in 1991, 20 years after it was founded. By 1994, revenue grew to $6 billion! Since 1994, Cardinal Health has made a number of acquisitions, expanding is spectrum of services in the pharmaceutical and health care industries. The company's acquisitions included Pyxis Corp. in automated supply and pharmaceutical dispensing, Owen Healthcare in hospital pharmacy management, Medicine Shoppe International in pharmacy franchising, R.P. Scherer Corp. and Automated Liquid Packaging in drug delivery formulation and contract manufacturing, PCI Services, Inc., in pharmaceutical packaging, Allegiance Corp. in medical-surgical product manufacturing and distribution, Bergen Brunswig's medical-surgical distribution to hospitals and care continuum, and Bindley Western in pharmaceutical distribution. By 2014, Cardinal Health had grown to $90 billion in revenue and 40 distribution centers.[16]

WHY THE HISTORY PERSPECTIVE OF THE BIG THREE?

The big three have a rich history of founders with vision, leaders with deep knowledge in the pharmaceutical, health care, and supply chain industries, and vast numbers of employees skilled at meeting the needs of patient care providers and providing safe pharmaceutical drugs to patients in need. Their revenue, employee, and asset numbers are impressive, to say the least. However, there is one statistic that despite their history and asset base, puts them at risk with potential structural changes from the Drug Quality and Security Act: their very low operating profit margins (Figure 5.3).

The operating profit margins for major pharmaceutical drug manufacturers in 2013 averaged 18.4%, and for generic drug manufacturers averaged 5.4%.[17] For fiscal 2014, the operating profit margin for McKesson was 1.72%, followed by Cardinal Health with 1.13% and AmerisourceBergen

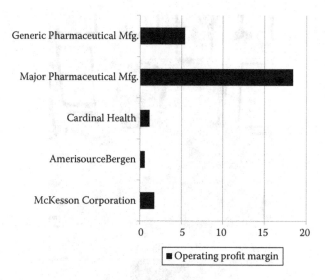

FIGURE 5.3
Operating profit margin. (From Charles Schwab Stock Research Summaries and http://yourbusiness.azcentral.com/average-profit-margin-pharmaceuticals-20671.html.)

with 0.58% Despite having massive revenue and asset bases, the big three have razor-thin operating profit margins.[18] Any added costs from changes through the Drug Quality and Security Act without compensatory price relief will send these large companies deep into red ink.

BACK TO STANDING IN LINE FOR A PRESCRIPTION

As I stand in line at my local Walmart pharmacy, a six-year-old girl said, "Look, Mommy, at all the pretty boxes!" What she was noticing was the many different totes in use by the Walmart pharmacy. The totes actually tell the supply chain story for the pharmacy as well.

This particular Walmart pharmacy uses red totes to receive high-value, time-sensitive pharmaceutical drugs from the McKesson distribution center. The red totes are also used for over-the-counter (OTC) drugs ordered from and delivered by McKesson. The orange totes are used by the Walmart distribution center for lower-valued drugs and orders that are not time sensitive (see Figure 5.4). It is part of a dual-sourcing strategy for the major pharmacy chains to use one of the big three for the higher-value, time-sensitive, and higher-risk pharmaceutical drugs, while using their

FIGURE 5.4
Walmart central fill orange tote. (From Jibu Abraham, pharmacy associate, Walmart pharmacy. Picture by Fred A. Kuglin. With permission.)

own forward distribution centers to handle the lower-value drugs and OTC medicines. My wife has a thyroxin generic drug prescription that is picked, packaged, and delivered to the Walmart pharmacy by the Walmart distribution center within 24 to 36 hours. It is picked up in a sealed packaged by my wife, without ever being handled by the local pharmacy. I am sure it came into the pharmacy in an orange tote! The yellow totes are used for refrigerated and temperature-controlled pharmaceutical drugs. A heavy-duty cardboard box (brown of course) is used to send expiring and recalled drugs to its return logistics provider, GENCO.[19]

The complexity to fill patient prescriptions at the local pharmacy, combined with the scale of servicing 230 million people as patients in the United States, places an enormous pressure on wholesale distributors to execute flawlessly.

THE DRUG QUALITY AND SECURITY ACT: WHOLESALE DISTRIBUTORS

Starting January 1, 2015, wholesale distributors must receive from the pharmaceutical drug manufacturers and provide to their customers transaction information, transaction history, and a transaction statement for all pharmaceutical drugs covered under the Drug Quality and Safety Act. The FDA is required to publish final guidance on the standards for interoperable data exchange to enhance secure tracing of products at the package level by November 27, 2022.

TRANSACTION INFORMATION AND TRANSACTION HISTORY

The transaction information being required by the FDA is the following:

- Proprietary or established name or names of the product
- Strength and dosage form of the product
- National Drug Code number of the product
- Container size
- Number of containers
- Lot number of the product
- Date of the transaction
- Date of the shipment, if more than 24 hours after the date of the transaction
- Business name and address of the person from whom and to whom ownership is being transferred[21]

Currently the wholesale distributors provide the majority of this information on pharmaceutical drugs to their pharmacy customers. For instance, according to Walmart, McKesson provides transaction information to Walmart on its invoices. What will be new is the placement of lot information and the National Drug Code number on the invoice. Walmart currently gets this information on the product itself directly from the pharmaceutical drug manufacturer.

The transaction history information being required is a statement in paper or electronic form including the transaction information for each prior transaction going back to the manufacturer of the product. Right now the wholesale distributors provide to their pharmacy customers only their own transactions. This will be a change for all wholesale distributors.[22]

The complexity of adding lot numbers and the National Drug Code to the transaction information may or may not be very significant for the wholesale distributors, depending upon their systems and current practices. What may be complex is adding the transaction history between the manufacturer and the wholesale distributor and encrypting it for proprietary reasons. The complexity of adding the transaction statement is still to be determined. It will be dependent on the standards developed by the FDA.

THE BIG THREE AND TECHNOLOGY

Throughout my career, I have had the pleasure of visiting multiple big three distribution centers (DCs). The size and complexity of one of these distribution centers is amazing. The average big three distribution center ships approximately $10 million per day in pharmaceutical drug sales to its customer pharmacies. When accounting for multiple states serviced by these DCs and multiple sizes of drug shipments, the number of stock-keeping units in one of these DCs can extend well beyond 100,000 in potential pharmaceutical drugs to ship to pharmacies.[23]

The DC receives the drugs in case/pallet quantities, places these cases/pallets into storage, and then pulls case quantities to its "order pick lanes." Random access storage is used to maximize the available storage in the DC. The order picker receives the orders from the customer pharmacies, picks the orders in the quantities needed, places the drugs in a tote, and closes out the order at the end of the pick lane. A manifest (that sometimes doubles as the invoice) is printed and attached to the outside of the tote. Totes are everywhere, or so it seems to a visitor.

In many of these DCs, the process is very automated. Wearable computer devices, such as those produced by Motorola Solutions, are used by warehouse personnel to scan and input all movement information within the warehouse. The information is transferred through a wireless local area network (LAN) to the network. This enables the tracking of inventory in real time from receiving, in-warehouse transfers, order picking, and shipment to pharmacy customers with a very high degree of accuracy. These devices can also update actual inventory information by SKU so that actual inventory matches the electronic inventory information. This feature enables pharmacy customers to go through online ordering systems, look up available inventory, and place orders with a high degree of confidence that their orders will be properly filled in a timely manner.[24] Regardless of how the Drug Supply Chain Security Act determines the big three as first, second, or third wholesale distributors, the use of wearable computer devices linked to an inventory-tracking network will enable the big three to comply with the new track and trace regulations.

THE OTHER 15%

According to Modern Distribution Management (MDM), the top pharmaceutical wholesale distributors after the big three are as follows[25]:

Morris & Dickson: $3.6 billion
H.D. Smith: $3.4 billion
Smith Drug: $2.2 billion
Curascript Specialty Distribution: $2.1 billion
NC Mutual Wholesale Drug: $1.1 billion
Anda Distribution: $1.0 billion

There is a significant drop-off in size from Cardinal Health to Morris & Dickson. However, I am still amazed as to the size of these wholesale distributors. In addition, some of these wholesale distributors have the same rich history in the pharmaceutical drug industry as their big three counterparts. For example, Morris & Dickson Co., LLC was founded in 1841 and today is owned and operated by the fifth generation of the Dickson family.[26]

WHOLESALE DISTRIBUTORS, REPACKAGING, AND THE DRUG QUALITY AND SECURITY ACT

Repackaging for wholesale distributors, especially the big three, is an integral part of their value-added services to retail pharmacies and hospitals.

Repackaging is defined as buying pharmaceutical drugs in bulk and repackaging the drugs with a pharmacy or hospital brand package. In some cases, the customized package has a specific number of doses or a specific use (i.e., the ICU, recovery room, etc.). The big three, such as McKesson and its McKesson RxPak program, leverage their buying power and offer these custom services with competitive pricing.[27]

With the new law, wholesale distributors will not only have to make sure they receive and pass on the prior ownership information, recall information, and quarantine information, but also be required to affix or imprint a product identifier on each package sold to pharmacies and hospitals. The only exception will be if the pharmaceutical drug has a standardized numerical identifier and the packaging with the identifier is not disturbed in the repackaging process. The specifics are still being worked out, and I am sure the wholesale distributors are working closely with the FDA to map out their repackaging processes with the new regulations to assess their new responsibilities. However, what I do know is that their repackaging operations will be impacted by the new law.[28]

TRANSACTION STATEMENT

There exist several areas that expose the pharmaceutical drug supply chain to product substitution, theft, and product diversion. One of the ways that the FDA is attempting to address these areas of exposure is through the transaction statement. The FDA is requiring a transaction statement to accompany the pharmaceutical drugs when transferring ownership in the supply chain. It is my understanding that this transaction statement will also be new for the wholesale distributors, although several of the items should not be new to them.

The FDA is requiring a statement, in paper or electronic form, that the entity transferring ownership in a transaction:

- Is authorized as required under Title II: Drug Supply Chain Security Act (DSCSA)
- Received the product from a person that is authorized as required under DSCSA
- Received transaction information and a transaction statement from the prior owner of the product, as required under the law
- Did not knowingly ship a suspect or illegitimate product

- Had systems and processes in place to comply with verification requirements under the law
- Did not knowingly provide false transaction information
- Did not knowingly alter the transaction history[29]

The first two are the anchors to the transaction statement. The wholesale distributor must be authorized as required under Title II of the DSCSA, and it must receive product from a person that is authorized as required under DSCSA. Let's take a look at a well-publicized case involving wholesale distributors substituting bad product for pharmaceutical drugs not even authorized by the FDA for sale in the United States.

PROBLEMS IN 2012

Despite the history and efforts by the wholesale distributors to provide safe and secure pharmaceutical drugs to patients, there are always people willing to do bad things to make money. The bad and ugly of wholesale distributors are exemplified by a situation in 2012 addressed by the FDA. Licensed wholesale distributors were caught by the FDA distributing counterfeit drugs and unapproved foreign-sourced oncology drugs.

On April 3, 2012, the FDA alerted health care professionals that a cancer drug, originating from a foreign source and purchased by U.S. medical practices, had been determined to be counterfeit. FDA lab tests confirmed that a counterfeit version of Roche's Altuzan 400 mg/16 ml (bevacizumab), an injectable cancer medication, was found in the United States and contained no active ingredient. Altuzan at the time was not approved by FDA for use in the United States but was an approved drug in Turkey. Medical practices obtained the counterfeit Altuzan and other unapproved products through foreign sources, in particular from Richards Pharma, also known as Richards Services, Warwick Healthcare Solutions, or Ban Dune Marketing, Inc. (BDMI). Many, if not all, of the products sold and distributed through this distributor have not been approved by the FDA. The agency cannot ensure that the manufacture and handling of these illegal products follows U.S. regulations, nor can the FDA ensure that these drugs are safe and effective for their intended uses.*[30]

---

* This information is from the FDA drug integrity and supply chain security website.

On April 25, 2012, the FDA issued letters to medical practices in the United States that purchased unapproved cancer medications from Quality Specialty Products (QSP) (also known as Montana Health Care Solutions), and distributed through Volunteer Distribution of Gainesboro, Tennessee, that may include counterfeit versions of Altuzan.[31]

On July 10, 2012, the FDA issued letters to medical practices in the United States that purchased unapproved medications that may include the counterfeit versions of Avastin or Altuzan. The medical practices purchased unapproved medications from foreign distributors such as Clinical Care, Quality Specialty Products, Montana Health Care Solutions, and Bridgewater Medical.[32]

Oncology drugs used to treat various forms of cancer. The National Cancer Institute has a list of cancer drug information summaries for patients and their loved ones to reference.[33] What is especially cruel in this case is that some cancers do respond to cancer drugs. A very good friend of mine had stage 3 lymphoma in the mid-1990s and beat the cancer with cancer drugs/treatments. The people who took these proscribed cancer drugs without active ingredients thought they were taking drugs that would help them. They lost precious time and had their cancers go untreated as a result of the fake drugs. The patients could have helped themselves by researching Altuzan and finding out it was not authorized for sale in the United States. In the end, it was a terrible scenario for these patients and their loved ones.

OTHER PROBLEMS

A friend of mine in law enforcement told me anonymously that most theft, substitution, and diversion of pharmaceutical drugs occur at the linkage points, or when the product physically changes hands. He told me the story of shipments from pharmaceutical companies that were stolen en route as truck drivers stopped at truck stops for dinner. The bad guys were alerted to the trailer number, the dispatch time, the route to the wholesale distributor DC, and the types of drugs being shipped by insiders at both the pharmaceutical manufacturer and the wholesale distributor. When the insiders were caught, new bad guys took their place. This time, the bad guys substituted bad product for good product while the truck drivers were at the truck stops. All they did was duplicate the packaging so the receiving department at the wholesale distributor DC would not detect the substitution. They also had duplicate seal numbers that matched the trailer manifest.

My friend also told me of truckloads of a popular erectile dysfunction drug being hijacked. The bad guys knew that there were stolen vehicle-tracking devices placed on the trailer (i.e., LoJack). They also knew that they had approximately 30 minutes before police would be notified and arrive at the scene. They would stop the tractor trailer, unload the shipment, split the shipment into four smaller shipments, and load the four smaller shipments onto four other trucks. The four smaller shipments would go into different directions. The bad guys would then reintroduce the erectile dysfunction drug back into the legitimate supply chain through willing wholesale distributors at 40% of the original cost. All the bad guys had to do was alter the pedigree paperwork to make everything look legitimate. The police would find the original tractor trailers, but the pharmaceutical drugs were long gone.

There were smaller examples described to me. In one situation, cartons of pain pills were being broken on purpose in transit. When the shipments would arrive at the wholesale distributor DC, the broken cartons would be refused by the wholesale distributor receiving department. The broken case would be repackaged and returned to the manufacturer. However, most of the pain pills would never make it back to the manufacturer. The driver and the receiving supervisor were working together, providing the pills to a local drug dealer.

SUMMARY

The pharmaceutical drug wholesale distributor industry is very large, with the dominant market share (85%) controlled by the big three: McKesson, AmerisourceBergen, and Cardinal Health. The industry as a whole has a rich history, with many companies tracing their origins to the 1800s and being led by pharmacists, doctors, and innovative risk-takers.

This industry has large revenues and asset bases but razor-thin operating margins. If their stockholders had it all over to do again, I am sure that many would deploy their investments into other industries that provide greater returns and less risk.

The Title II: Drug Supply Chain Security Act is intended to secure the supply chain through mandating transaction information, transaction history, and a transaction statement for pharmaceutical drugs as they change ownership from manufacturer to the patient or consumer. Depending on the final standards developed and issued by the FDA, system changes will potentially be needed for the wholesale distributors to comply with this law. With its razor-thin margins, any increase in costs will have to be offset by productivity improvements or compensatory price relief.

The wholesale distributors participating in repackaging programs for pharmacies and hospitals will have to comply with the new regulations. These regulations are placing repackagers and pharmaceutical drug manufacturers in the same group, and rightfully so. They are "originating" the packaging of the pharmaceutical drugs, and need to affix unique product identifiers to the packaging. This will add cost and complexity to their repackaging operations.

The FDA is in a dilemma. About a decade ago, the FDA issued a report titled *Profiling of the Prescription Drug Wholesaling Industry: Examination of the Entities Defining Supply and Demand in Drug Distribution—Final Report*. In this report, the FDA refers to the "big five" full-line wholesale distributors that comprised 90% of the drug sales in the United States in 1999. These five wholesale distributors were McKesson HBOC, Inc., Bergen Brunswig Drug Company, Cardinal Health, Inc., AmeriSource Corporation, and Bindley Western Drug Company. Since the year 2000, AmeriSource Corporation and Bergen Brunswig Drug Company merged to form AmerisourceBergen, and Cardinal Health bought Bindley Western Drug Company, forming the big three. Any significant increase in costs could drive one of the big three out of business, into bankruptcy, or into a merger with another one of the big three, furthering the definition of an oligopoly in the marketplace.[34]

In my introduction, I discussed how the pharmaceutical industry employs 2 million people. If 99% are good, law-abiding people, this leaves 20,000 people, or "the bad guys and gals," to do bad things. In my opinion, most of these bad things happen at the linkage points, or outside the wholesale distributor distribution centers. We must do what we can to protect patient safety and combat diversion, substitution of drugs, and tampering throughout the supply chain. Some industry insiders call it the secure supply chain. However, we must also be smart and ensure that we can protect the supply chain partners from stifling regulation, keeping them in business so they can supply the needed pharmaceutical drugs to patients and customers. It is a delicate balance that the FDA must chart to successfully implement the Drug Quality and Safety Act.

ENDNOTES

1. American Pharmacy Association, telephone call, July 29, 2014.
2. Alexander Gaffney, How Many Drugs Has FDA Approved in Its Entire History?, RAPS, 2014, http://www.raps.org/Regulatory-Focus/News/2014/10/03/20488/How-Many-Drugs-has-FDA-Approved-in-its-Entire-History-New-Paper-Explains/.
3. MDM 2013 Market Leaders, Top Pharmaceuticals Distributors, MDM, http://www.mdm.com/2013_pharmaceuticals_mdm-market-leaders.
4. Adam J. Fein, 2013–14 Economic Report on Pharmaceutical Wholesalers and Specialty Distributors, 2013, http://drugchannelsinstitute.com/files/2013-14-PharmaceuticalWholesalers-Overview.pdf; discussion with VP pharmacy operations, major pharmacy retail chain, July 30, 2014.
5. MDM 2013 Market Leaders, Top Pharmaceuticals Distributors, MDM, http://www.mdm.com/2013_pharmaceuticals_mdm-market-leaders.
6. Charles Schwab stock research summary for MCK, ABC, and CAH, July 29, 2014.
7. Ibid.
8. http://www.mckesson.com/about-mckesson/our-history/.
9. Ibid.
10. Creating a Healthier Future, Annual Report, McKesson, 2014, p. 7, http://investor.mckesson.com/sites/mckesson.investorhq.businesswire.com/files/report/file/McKesson_2014_Annual_Report.pdf.
11. http://www.fundinguniverse.com/company-histories/bergen-brunswig-corporation-history/.
12. Ibid.
13. Ibid.
14. http://www.amerisourcebergen.com/abcnew/about.aspx.
15. http://cardinalhealth.com/us/en/aboutus/ourhistory.
16. Ibid.
17. Tiffany C. Wright, The Average Profit Margin of Pharmaceuticals, AZ Central, http://yourbusiness.azcentral.com/average-profit-margin-pharmaceuticals-20671.html.
18. Charles Schwab stock research summary for MCK, ABC, and CAH, July 29, 2014.
19. Personal visit to local Walmart pharmacy, July 30, 2014.
20. Drug Supply Chain Security Act (DSCSA) Implementation Plan, FDA, http://www.fda.gov/Drugs/DrugSafety/DrugIntegrityandSupplyChainSecurity/DrugSupplyChainSecurityAct/ucm382022.htm.
21. Ibid.
22. Ibid.
23. Charles Schwab stock research summary for MCK, ABC, and CAH, July 29, 2014.
24. http://www.motorolasolutions.com/US-EN/Home.
25. MDM 2013 Market Leaders, Top Pharmaceuticals Distributors, MDM, http://www.mdm.com/2013_pharmaceuticals_mdm-market-leaders.
26. https://www.morrisdickson.com/.

27. http://www.mckesson.com/pharmacies/mail-order/packaging-programs/packaging-programs/.
28. H.R. 3204—Drug Quality and Security Act, Congress.gov, https://www.congress.gov/bill/113th-congress/house-bill/3204.
29. Ilisa B.G. Bernstein, Getting Ready for the Drug Supply Chain Security Act (Title II of the Drug Quality and Security Act), presented at Association of Food and Drug Officials Education Conference, June 13, 2014, p. 7.
30. Another Counterfeit Cancer Medicine Found in U.S.—Illegal Practice Puts Patients at Risk, FDA, 2012, http://www.fda.gov/Drugs/DrugSafety/DrugIntegrity andSupplyChainSecurity/ucm298047.htm.
31. Ibid.
32. Ibid.
33. A to Z List of Cancer Drugs, National Cancer Institute, http://www.cancer.gov/cancertopics/druginfo/alphalist.
34. Profile of the Prescription Drug Wholesaling Industry, FDA, http://www.fda.gov/ohrms/dockets/dockets/05n0403/05n-0403-bkg0001-04-05-3.pdf.

6

The Customer/Patient Touchpoint—
Literally and Electronically:
Internet Pharmacies, Pill Mills,
and Other Lurking Dangers

OVERVIEW

In Chapter 5, we were left standing in line, waiting for our prescription to be filled by the pharmacist. There are many sick people waiting in line, and the pharmacists and their assistants are working very hard to fill everyone's prescription. There are multiple ways that a customer or patient can get a prescription filled.

The most common way is to have the prescription sent to the pharmacy by the doctor or nurse and to have the patient pick up the needed pharmaceutical drugs. Patients can also use mail-order pharmacies. Mail-order pharmacies are usually associated with insurers or retail pharmacies. The doctor or nurse sends the prescription to the mail-order pharmacies, and the pharmaceutical drugs are delivered to you by mail. The drugs may cost less by mail, but it does take time. People who take pharmaceutical drugs on a regular basis for long-term problems (e.g., my wife and her levothyroxine, my friend's Parkinson's medications) are good candidates to use mail-order pharmacies. It may go without saying that short-term medication needs and temperature-controlled medications (the yellow tote medications) should go through a traditional pharmacy.

Another alternative for the patient/customer is to use an Internet or online pharmacy. Both the mail-order pharmacies and Internet or online pharmacies take prescriptions electronically and mail the pharmaceutical drugs to the patient. The big difference is that an Internet or online pharmacy is almost always not associated with an insurer or retail pharmacy.

DRUG QUALITY AND SECURITY ACT AND LOCAL PHARMACIES

In doing research for this chapter, I contacted regional pharmacy managers for three of the top pharmacy retail chains. In all three cases, I was informed of the same response they have to the Drug Supply Chain Security Act (Title II of the Drug Quality and Security Act). These three regional managers said they would do what the Food and Drug Administration (FDA) wants, and negotiate any net add-in costs with the pharmacy benefits managers (PBMs). This means that patients will pay more—through either higher premiums or higher co-pays.

These regional pharmacy managers also said they will do everything possible to minimize the impact of this law on the local pharmacists and their assistants. This makes sense, because the beehive of activity in a pharmacy can be worrisome without the appropriate technology to simplify their activities. As I mentioned in Chapter 5, some of these pharmacies fill up to 600 prescriptions a day. All prescriptions must be properly filled, because the patient's safety is at risk with each and every prescription.

One representative from the FDA (who wished to remain anonymous) told me the FDA was not worried about compliance of the large pharmacy chains with the new law beyond the miscellaneous theft, occasional internal security incidents, and their interaction with "pill mills." This representative said they were very worried about Internet or online pharmacies. Let's take a deep dive into the world of Internet or online pharmacies and see why the FDA is so concerned.

PHARMACY PRESCRIPTION ORDER-FILL PROCESS

The pharmacy prescription order-fill process starts with a physician authorizing a prescription to be filled for a patient. This doctor-to-patient relationship is very important for many reasons. The exposure to overdoses of medications, drug interactions (both active and inert ingredients), and the proper diagnosis of conditions all come into play for patient safety.

The physician (or as I stated earlier, the nurse authorized by the physician) will approve a prescription for a patient and send the authorized prescription to both the pharmacy and the pharmacy benefits manager. The pharmacy benefits manager will approve the prescription and inform the pharmacy of the charges to be collected from the patient. These charges range from a $4 co-pay to hundreds of dollars. The pharmacists at the pharmacy are licensed by their state boards of pharmacy, and must renew their licenses on a regular basis.

The pharmacy will order the pharmaceutical drugs for this prescription from its wholesale distributor (or forward distribution center). The wholesale distributor (or forward distribution center) will order the drugs from the pharmaceutical manufacturer. The wholesale distributor and the pharmaceutical manufacturer are (and with the new Drug Quality and Security Act must be) registered with the FDA and in compliance with the FDA regulations. Although the state boards of pharmacy have direct oversight of the pharmacies, the FDA has oversight of the activities of the actual dispensing of the drugs (see Figure 6.1).

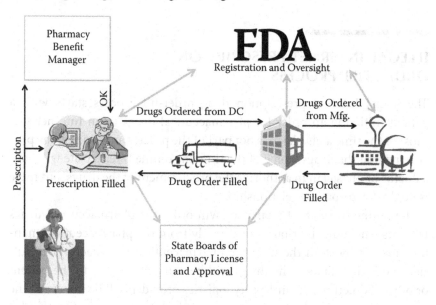

FIGURE 6.1
Pharmacy prescription order-fill process, simple view.

LEGAL ONLINE PRESCRIPTION ORDER-FILL PROCESS

The legal online prescription order-fill process has many similarities to its brick-and-mortar counterpart. The prescription order-fill process starts with a physician authorizing a prescription to be filled for a patient. The physician (or the nurse authorized by the physician) will approve a prescription for a patient and send the authorized prescription to the online pharmacy and the pharmacy benefits manager. The pharmacy benefits manager will approve the prescription and inform the online pharmacy of the charges to be collected from the patient.

The pharmacy will order the pharmaceutical drugs for this prescription directly from the pharmaceutical manufacturer (or at times the wholesale distributor). The wholesale distributor and the pharmaceutical manufacturer are usually registered with the FDA and in compliance with the FDA regulations. If the pharmaceutical manufacturer is a foreign manufacturer, it will also be registered and approved by the FDA. The pharmaceutical drugs will be shipped, cleared through Customs, and delivered direct to the patient. The doctor-to-patient relationship and the FDA registration and oversight of the supply chain participants remain intact (see Figure 6.2).

ILLEGAL INTERNET PRESCRIPTION ORDER-FILL PROCESS

The illegal Internet prescription drug order-fill process starts with a patient initiating an order for pharmaceutical drugs to an Internet site. Most of the time a physician is not part of the process authorizing the procurement of the drugs. Some of the time the online Internet site will have a doctor or physician to authorize the procurement of the drugs, but there is no doctor-to-patient relationship.

The online or Internet pharmacy will order the pharmaceutical drugs from its wholesale distributor or directly from the pharmaceutical manufacturer. Almost all the time the pharmaceutical manufacturer is outside the United States. The drugs will be shipped directly to the patient or buyer. Sometimes a third-party logistics provider will be involved. The Internet site, the international pharmaceutical drug manufacturer, and if used, the wholesale distributor or third-party logistics provider will be absent of any FDA regulation (see Figure 6.3).

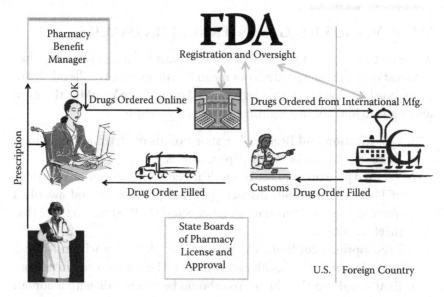

FIGURE 6.2
Legal Internet pharmacy order-fill process, simple view.

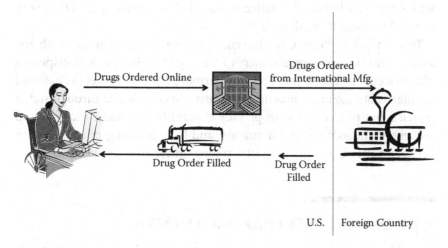

FIGURE 6.3
Illegal Internet pharmacy order-fill process, simple view.

LEGAL VERSUS ILLEGAL INTERNET PHARMACIES

As we just covered in the above summaries, just because a pharmacy has a market over the Internet does not mean it is illegitimate or illegal. There are online pharmacies that are legitimate. According to WebMD, there are four signs to look for in a legitimate pharmacy website:

1. **U.S. location and license.** The state boards of pharmacy have high standards for the licensing of pharmacies.
2. **Verified pharmacy practice site.** The National Association of Boards of Pharmacy˚ (NABP) inspects Internet pharmacies and awards a Verified Internet Pharmacy Practice Sites˝ (VIPPS) seal to those that meet its criteria.
3. **Prescription required.** Any trustworthy pharmacy will insist on a prescription from a health care provider who has seen you in person.
4. **Real people on the phone.** You should be able to talk with a human being, including a licensed pharmacist, to answer questions about your prescription.[1]

Regarding the second point, the National Association of Boards of Pharmacy has a process to inspect and award its VIPPS seal. The good news is that the NABP has reviewed over 10,000 Internet pharmacy sites. The bad news is that only 3% of these Internet sites appear to be in compliance with pharmacy laws and practice standards. Ninety-seven percent of the Internet sites reviewed by NABP were deemed not in compliance with pharmacy laws and practice standards![2] No wonder the FDA is very concerned about these sites.

To earn a VIPPS seal, an Internet pharmacy must comply with the survey and licensing requirements of every state in which it dispenses pharmaceutical drugs. The Internet pharmacy must also meet the national standards of pharmacy practice, demonstrate compliance through stated policies and procedures with privacy standards, and authentication and security standards and requirements, and have meaningful consultation between patients and pharmacists, among others.[3]

WHY DO INTERNET PHARMACIES EXIST?

Illegal Internet pharmacies are easy to set up. One law enforcement person in the Northeast said they are like dandelions popping up in an early spring lawn. When you pull one up, several more spring up to take its place.

For a quick test, I chose two popular pharmaceutical drugs that are ordered online: Viagra and hydrocodone. I chose Viagra because of the cost. One 100 mg Viagra tablet at Walgreens or Walmart costs $29.67, while at CVS it costs $31.60.[4] When I inquired on how to buy Viagra cheaply (using two search engines), I found several Internet pharmacies willing to sell Viagra 100 mg tablets between $8.00 and $20.00 per tablet. The biggest advertisement by each of these Internet pharmacies was "no prescription necessary."

Next I inquired about hydrocodone. Before and immediately after my neck surgery my primary care physician put me on hydrocodone for pain. I used 325 mg–10 mg acetaminophen/hydrocodone tablets. The cost was $13.45 for 20 tablets at my local pharmacy. They were the same price at Walmart.[5] (Despite the excruciating pain, I refused to be "upgraded" to oxycodone because I don't like the potential of getting reliant on pain pills.) Once again, I found several Internet pharmacies willing to sell 325 mg–10 mg acetaminophen/hydrocodone tablets for $6.40 for 20 tablets with "no prescription necessary."

It is obvious from these two examples that two of the biggest reasons why illegal Internet pharmacies exist are cost and "no prescription necessary." Remembering the WebMD advice on getting a real person on the phone, I decided to call one of the Internet pharmacies that posted a telephone number on its website. It was a Canadian Internet pharmacy, and a young lady immediately answered the phone. Needless to say, I was surprised by the honesty and brazen openness of this representative.

I posed as a potential customer, and asked about Viagra and hydrocodone. She mentioned the approximate prices I identified earlier. When I asked about countries of origin of these drugs, she replied they could come from Canada, Australia, New Zealand, Turkey, India, Singapore, and surprisingly, the United States. I asked her how they could sell their drugs for so much less. She said they operate in Canada, outside the burdensome regulations of the FDA and the boards of pharmacy in 50 states. When I inquired about speaking with a physician, she said she could make one available at my request, but a prescription was not necessary. I asked about the quality of the drugs. She said if I was not satisfied, I could return the container for a full refund. However, she reminded me of the astounding reviews they have received from satisfied customers. (I had visions of college students staying up through the night writing the fake reviews to support her customer satisfaction score!)

There are significant downsides to buying drugs that do not have the right mix of active ingredients, do not have any active ingredients, or have different inert ingredients that pose drug interaction problems for patients. For this Internet pharmacy, all risk is clearly assumed by the buyer. This includes financial risk! There are many rumors that these illegal Internet pharmacies sell your financial information (MasterCard, Visa, or other payment information) to third parties to use in the black market.

It was obvious that this Canadian pharmacy did not have a U.S. location, was not a verified pharmacy practice site, and did not require a prescription from a physician. It did have a real person, so this Internet pharmacy scored one out of four on the WebMD four signs for legitimacy for Internet pharmacy sites.

THE FDA, THE U.S. JUSTICE DEPARTMENT, AND INTERNET PHARMACIES

Even before the Drug Quality and Security Act, the FDA and the U.S Justice Department were trying to combat illegal Internet pharmacies. On August 25, 2011, the *Wall Street Journal* reported that Google agreed to pay $500 million to avoid Justice Department prosecution on charges that it knowingly accepted illegal advertisements from Canadian online pharmacies for years.[6] Stopping the ads and the support targeting consumers in the United States is certainly one step in the right direction.

As my example showed, using search engines to inquire about Internet pharmacies and the buying of prescription drugs online still resulted in a slew of Internet pharmacy sites being referenced. Certainly, more was and still is needed to inhibit access to these drugs.

THE DRUG QUALITY AND SECURITY ACT AND ILLEGAL INTERNET PHARMACIES

As we discussed in Chapter 4, the Drug Quality and Security Act requires that supply chain participants set up the proper systems to verify a product identifier for every pharmaceutical drug package they handle. All supply chain participants are now required by law to quarantine and investigate any pharmaceutical drug that has been identified as suspect. If any pharmaceutical drug is found to be illegitimate through investigation, the FDA and other supply chain participants are to be notified.[7]

On May 22, 2014, the FDA issued a news release that the FDA, the U.S. Customs and Border Protection (CBP), and U.S.-based international mail facilities cooperated in extensive examinations of imported pharmaceutical drug packages. Most of the examined packages contained illegal prescription drugs that had been ordered from online sources or Internet pharmacies.[8]

In conjunction with INTERPOL and in support of the seventh annual International Internet Week of Action (IIWA), authorities from 111 countries collaborated to identify the makers and distributors of illegal pharmaceutical drugs and medical devices that used the Internet. Their efforts resulted in the detention and seizure of 19,618 packages. These packages supposedly contained unapproved and counterfeit drugs from Australia, the United Kingdom, New Zealand, and Canada, but in reality contained drugs from India, China, Singapore, Taiwan, Mexico, Laos, and Malaysia, in addition to Australia, New Zealand, and the UK.[9]

At least the FDA is trying to address illegal Internet pharmacies. However, if it was this easy to detect illegal pharmaceutical drugs and medical devices, the obvious question is, why isn't it done on an ongoing basis? The answer is partially rooted in the sheer scale and volume of packages an international mail center handles on a daily basis. Several years ago I had the pleasure to visit a major U.S. Postal Service sorting facility next to a large international airport. The international mail was sorted and sent to the CBP for processing. The volume of mail was incredible and appeared to be overwhelming!

The CBP and the FDA do have a process to legally import prescription drugs into the United States, although as a general rule, the FDA does not allow prescription drugs to be mailed to the United States.[10] Both agencies said that interested parties should be referred to the FDA import/export team and review the FDA Regulatory Procedures Manual for Importations for more information.[11] One CBP agent at the Dallas–Ft. Worth airport (he referred to himself as just another "blue shirt") said it would be best to have pharmaceutical drugs sent by a courier service with a letter from the physician prescribing the drugs to accompany the package. This way the package can be flagged, and the courier's U.S. Customs broker can inform the FDA about the package.

WHY A COURIER SERVICE?

A courier service familiar with U.S. Customs laws will know how to legally import pharmaceutical drugs. Areas that the courier service will have to address are the Customs entry process, Customs bond requirements, the U.S. import documentation, the Harmonized Tariff Schedule (HTS) classification of the pharmaceutical drugs, the FDA import product codes, the FDA import affirmation of compliance codes, the FDA prior notice and establishment of a separate account, and the use of the Import Trade Auxiliary Communication System (ITACS).[12]

ILLEGAL INTERNET PHARMACIES AND COURIER SERVICES

One of the best courier services, FedEx Corporation, was indicted in July 2014 for conspiracy to distribute controlled substances, conspiracy to distribute misbranded drugs, and distribution of controlled substances and misbranded drugs. On August 15, 2014, the Justice Department added conspiracy to launder money in conjunction with the distribution of pharmaceutical drugs from illegal Internet pharmacies on a "collect on delivery" basis. FedEx pleaded not guilty and is fighting these charges.[13]

It is apparent that significant numbers of deliveries were made from Internet pharmacies with invalid or nonexistent prescriptions. Some of these shipments were destined for empty lots or vacant homes. According to Patrick Fitzgerald, FedEx senior vice president of marketing and communications, FedEx handles 10 million packages a day! The challenge to monitor every one of them is next to impossible.[14] I have been to two FedEx facilities during my career (Memphis and Louisville) and can attest to the massive scale and volume that each one of these facilities handles. It is easy to see how an efficient supply chain built for size and speed can be exploited at times by illegal operations.

BACK TO THE DRUG QUALITY AND SECURITY ACT AND THE FFDCA

We will certainly let the judicial process sort out all the particulars in this case. In my opinion, the FDA should provide FDA-approved couriers with a list of known illegal Internet pharmacies so they can prescreen shipments and address them with the proper authorities.

The FDA established its Secure Supply Chain Pilot Program in 2013 to enhance the security of imported drugs. This program was launched with the participation of 13 companies prequalified by the agency and up to five selected drug products. The objective is to prevent the importation of unapproved, adulterated, or misbranded drugs. The FDA is cooperating with CBP and sharing information about the participants and the selected drug shipments.[15]

According to a February 21, 2014, publication by Sandler, Strauss and Rosenberg P.A., the companies accepted into the program are Above, Inc., Allergen, Inc., Estella's U.S. Technologies, Inc., Bristol-Myers Squibb Company, Colene Corporation, GE Healthcare, Inc., GlaxoSmithKline LLC, Merck Sharp & Dome Corporation, Milan Pharmaceuticals, Inc., Novartis Pharmaceuticals Corporation, Pfizer, Inc., Tea Pharmaceuticals USA, Inc., and Watson Laboratories, Inc. In this publication, Sandler, Strauss and Rosenberg said that according to the FDA, each of these companies has committed to comply with requirements of the Federal Food, Drug, and Cosmetic Act (FFDCA), has a validated secure supply chain protocol per the Customs-Trade Partnership Against Terrorism, has a plan in place to quickly correct potential problems the FDA identifies regarding importation of specific products, has effective recall and corrective action plans in place, and maintains control over its drugs from the time of manufacture abroad through entry into the United States.[16]

All of this is positive. However, where are the couriers? They are the Customs brokers and the transport providers. They are the ones actually handling the pharmaceutical drug shipments. They are the ones that will be responsible for the quarantine of suspected proscribed shipments, execute any recalls, and institute corrective actions necessary throughout the supply chain. I understand they provide a "service for hire" with the major pharmaceutical companies (especially the ones in the Secure Supply Chain Pilot Program). However, once the pharmaceutical drug shipments leave the manufacturer's shipping dock, it is the courier's responsibility to handle the shipment and all administrative activities supporting the shipment to the final destination. Top-tier couriers like FedEx have 160,000 employees in offices in 220 countries![17] In my opinion, embracing the top couriers as part of the solution sure seems preferable over treating them as part of the problem.

PILL MILLS

A pill mill is a doctor, health care facility, or clinic that prescribes or dispenses controlled prescription drugs (controlled substances) outside the scope of the prevailing standards of medical practice or violates state laws regarding the prescribing or dispensing of controlled prescription drugs.[18] Florida was a haven for pill mills for many years.

My parents retired in Florida and had many retired friends with medical ailments. I remembered a few of their friends visiting pain management clinics on a frequent basis, while a neighbor suffered from depression after losing his wife of 60 years and visited a local clinic for antidepressant medications. A popular topic of conversation during their bridge games was what medications everyone was taking for their ailments. Controlled prescription drugs always seemed available for the asking. At the time, I didn't think anything of it because these people were in their 80s and at the tail end of their lives.

By 2010, according to Florida attorney general Pam Bondi, Florida led the nation in diverted prescription drugs. Seven Floridians were dying every day of prescription drug overdoses. Florida had weak regulatory oversight of pain management practices, limited oversight of physician-dispensing habits, and no statewide Prescription Drug Monitoring Program (PDMP).[19]

In 2011, Florida passed its Anti-Pill Mill Bill. The state instituted stronger regulatory oversight of pain management practices and physician-dispensing habits, and now has a PDMP. These measures worked! In 2010, there were more than 900 registered pain management clinics in Florida. As of January 2014, there were only 367 registered pain management clinics in Florida. In 2010, the Drug Enforcement Administration (DEA), through its Automation of Reports and Consolidated Orders System (ARCOS), reported that 98 of the top 100 oxycodone-dispensing physicians in the nation were located in Florida. In 2014, this number was down to zero.[20]

There are ways to recognize pill mills. These doctors, health care facilities, or clinics will usually accept cash only and not insurance. No appointments are necessary, and they usually have poor to no medical records. Physical examinations may not be performed, and they typically dispense large prescription doses of controlled substances that exceed the boundaries of acceptable medical care.[21]

In my opinion, the Drug Quality and Security Act and its track and trace regulations will help reduce the number of pill mills. Through the use of product identifiers and the reporting of the transaction history and transaction statements, the FDA, with the state law enforcement agencies, can track large dispensers of controlled substances and shut them down when violations are discovered.

LOCAL PHARMACIES AND PILL MILLS

According to one pharmacist who manages a major retail chain pharmacy, some of the oversight of pill mills may come back on pharmacists' shoulders. As the new track and trace regulations are implemented, it is expected that pill mills will do less dispensing but more prescribing of controlled substances. These prescriptions will have to be filled by a state-licensed pharmacist. Some of this oversight is already taking place. A few of the large pharmacy chains are monitoring the levels of controlled substances dispensed by pharmacy stores in order to detect spikes in volume. This puts pressure on the pharmacists to detect spikes in prescriptions by doctor, by pain clinics, or by medical facility. According to this pharmacy manager, since pharmacies will be the "customer touchpoint" and filling the prescriptions, they will be called upon by the appropriate law enforcement personnel to produce any and all abuse details.

CVS PHARMACY IN SANFORD, FLORIDA

The pharmacy manager was referring specifically to the two CVS pharmacies in Sanford, Florida. According to articles in the *Orlando Sentinel*, the pharmacist-in-charge at one of the pharmacies told federal drug agents that customers would ask for "the Ms" or "the blues"—street slang for the painkiller oxycodone. He also said he didn't think such a request was suspicious, despite the reported facts that customers lived in Kentucky, obtained their prescriptions from South Florida doctors, and then filled their prescriptions in Sanford.[22]

Paul Doering, a professor at the University of Florida's College of Pharmacy who was asked to review the case for the government, opined that there were red flags when customers who lived out of state came into the Sanford stores. He said he could not "foresee any explanation for this set of red flags that would satisfy my professional obligation not to fill the scripts."[23]

Despite the suspicious circumstances, the pharmacists filled prescriptions for millions of oxycodone pills in recent years. CVS's misconduct at the two Sanford pharmacies was deemed so egregious by U.S. drug enforcement administrator Michele Leonhart that she banned the pharmacies from dispensing controlled substances—which include OxyContin, Vicodin, Ritalin, and Xanax, among others. This effort was part of the state of Florida and Attorney General Pam Bondi's ongoing efforts to curb Florida's prescription drug epidemic.[24]

WALGREENS SETTLEMENT

On June 11, 2013, it was reported that the DEA reached an $80 million settlement with Walgreens over rule violations that allowed tens of thousands of units of powerful painkillers such as oxycodone to illegally wind up in the hands of drug addicts and dealers. Mark R. Trouville, chief of the U.S. DEA's Miami field office, said Walgreens committed numerous record-keeping and dispensing violations of the Controlled Substances Act at a major East Coast distribution center in Jupiter, Florida, and at six retail pharmacies around the state. The drugs also included hydrocodone and Xanax. Authorities said the Jupiter center failed to flag suspicious orders of drugs it received from pharmacies, and the retail outlets routinely filled prescriptions that clearly were not for a legitimate medical use.[25]

CVS Pharmacy and Walgreens are well-run pharmacy chains with excellent reputations. In my opinion, the 1% rule I identified in my introduction certainly came into play in both of these cases. CVS has approximately 200,000 employees in 45 states, Puerto Rico, and the District of Columbia,[26] while Walgreens has approximately 240,000 employees.[27] One percent "bad employees" still amounts to 4,400 "bad people" within these two pharmacy chains. In my opinion, the FDA and the DEA should focus on the policies and procedures to inhibit the 1%, as the state of Florida did with its Pill Mill Bill. These efforts with CVS and Walgreens have had reverberation through other pharmacy chains, as my pharmacy manager source can attest!

SUMMARY

Title II: Supply Chain Security Act of the Drug Quality and Security Act will help improve the security of the pharmacy prescription order-fill process. With the explosion of the use of the Internet for shopping, it is understandable that computer-literate people will turn to online or Internet pharmacies for their pharmaceutical drugs. However, only 3% of the online or Internet pharmacies are legitimate!

The risks associated with illegal online Internet pharmacies include buying fake pharmaceutical drugs that are ineffective or dangerous. The lure of cheaper drugs from an illegal Internet pharmacy is great, as we pointed out in our hydrocodone and Viagra examples. However, the downside risks are significant, especially with pain pills and high-impact pharmaceutical drugs such as oncology drugs. In addition, identity theft is a high possibility with these foreign-based illegal Internet pharmacies. Providing any payment information to them may expose an unsuspecting consumer to financial loss.

As for the pill mills, wholesale distributors and pharmacies are now required to produce transaction information, the transaction history, and a transaction statement when ownership of pharmaceutical drugs changes hands. A spike in the ordering volume of controlled substances by any supply chain entity or consumer (individual, medical facility, clinic, doctor, etc.) dictates the need for both wholesale distributors and pharmacists to report the information to the FDA and the appropriate law enforcement agencies.

WebMD and the FDA have wonderful websites that identify the answers to frequently asked questions regarding Internet pharmacies. My recommendation regarding ordering pharmaceutical drugs over the Internet is "buyer beware," and you should refer to these websites when you may be inclined to use them. If you are an employee with a wholesale distributor or pharmacy, my recommendation is to report anything suspicious, like a spike in demand from an ordering entity or person. Keeping drugs off the street or out of the hands of abusers of prescription drugs will save lives—and maybe your job as well!

ENDNOTES

1. Kara Mayer Robinson, Online and Mail-Order Medicine: How to Buy Safely, WebMD, 2015, http://www.webmd.com/healthy-aging/features/beyond-the-pharmacy-online-and-mail-order-prescription-drugs.
2. VIPPS, NABP, http://www.nabp.net/programs/accreditation/vipps.
3. Ibid.
4. Mary Hiers, Cost of Buying Viagra at CVS, Walgreens, and Walmart Pharmacy, AccessRx, 2012, http://www.accessrx.com/blog/erectile-dysfunction/viagra/cost-of-buying-viagra-at-cvs-walgreens-and-walmart-pharmacy/.
5. http://www.goodrx.com/hydrocodone-acetaminophen.
6. Thomas Catan, Google Forks over Settlement on Rx Ads, *The Wall Street Journal*, 2011, http://online.wsj.com/news/articles/SB10001424053111904787404576528332418595052.
7. FDA Begins Implementation of Drug Quality and Security Act, Center for Safe Internet Pharmacies, 2014, http://www.safemedsonline.org/2014/05/fda-begins-implementation-of-drug-quality-and-security-act/; Chapter 4.
8. FDA Targets Illegal Online Pharmacies in Globally Coordinated Action, FDA, http://www.fda.gov/NewsEvents/Newsroom/PressAnnouncements/ucm398499.htm.
9. Ibid.
10. Regulatory Procedures Manual, FDA, http://www.fda.gov/iceci/compliancemanuals/regulatoryproceduresmanual/default.htm.
11. Import Operations and Actions, Regulatory Procedures Manual, FDA, http://www.fda.gov/downloads/ICECI/ComplianceManuals/RegulatoryProceduresManual/UCM074300.pdf.
12. Import Trade Auxiliary Communication System, FDA, http://www.fda.gov/ForIndustry/ImportProgram/ucm296314.htm.
13. Laura Stevens, FedEx Faces Additional Charges in Prescription-Drug Delivery Case, *The Wall Street Journal*, 2014, http://online.wsj.com/articles/fedex-faces-additional-charges-in-prescription-drug-delivery-case-1408145975.
14. Ibid.
15. FDA Initiates the Secure Supply Chain Pilot Program to Enhance Security of Imported Drugs, NABP, 2014, https://www.nabp.net/news/fda-initiates-the-secure-supply-chain-pilot-program-to-enhance-security-of-imported-drugs.
16. Travis Sandler and Rosenberg Trade Report, Secure Supply Chain Pilot Program for Imported Drugs Gets Underway, ST&R, 2014, http://www.strtrade.com/news-publications-FDA-import-drug-secure-supply-chain-022114.html.
17. http://about.van.fedex.com/fedex_express.

18. Pill Mill Initiative, Office of the Attorney General of Florida, http://myfloridalegal. com/pages.nsf/Main/AA7AAF5CAA22638D8525791B006A30C8.
19. Ibid.
20. Ibid.
21. Ibid.
22. Amy Pavuk, Rx for Danger: DEA Blasts CVS for Ignoring "Red Flags" at Sanford Stores, *Orlando Sentinel*, 2012, http://articles.orlandosentinel.com/2012-10-28/news/ os-cvs-dea-oxycodone-ban-20121028_1_sanford-cvs-sanford-pharmacies-sanford- stores.
23. Ibid.
24. Ibid.
25. Curt Anderson, Walgreens Settles Painkiller Case with DEA for $80 Million, *Daily Finance*, 2013, http://www.dailyfinance.com/2013/06/11/walgreens-settles-painkiller- case-dea/.
26. http://info.cvscaremark.com/about-us.
27. http://www.walgreens.com/topic/companyhelp/company_help_main.jsp.

7

When Things Go Bump in the Night: Reverse Logistics

OVERVIEW

Title II of the Drug Quality and Security Act (DQSA) is designed to address the supply chain from manufacturer to customer or patient. This works well most of the time. In a perfect pharmaceutical supply chain world, there is no illegitimate product to quarantine, no damaged product, no recalled product, and no damaged cases in transit. However, this theoretical optimum scenario doesn't exist. As in the Scottish prayer in *the Cornish and West Country Litany* (1926), "things that go bump in the night" do in fact happen.[1] (The people who do bad things may not be "goulies and ghosties and long-leggedy beasties," as in the prayer and adopted by Dr. Seuss, among others, but they are for sure a different form of monster.) When things do occur out of the ordinary, these pharmaceutical drugs must go somewhere, because as we discussed earlier in the book, the physical space within a retail pharmacy store is quite small. Many people think that these drugs are sent back to the manufacturer. Sometimes this happens, but most of the time the drugs are sent to a pharmaceutical drug reverse logistics provider called a reverse distributor.

WHAT IS REVERSE LOGISTICS?

Reverse logistics (or reverse distribution) is just that, the supply chain in reverse. In the forward supply chain, pharmaceutical drugs flow from the manufacturer to the customer or patient. The payment for the pharmaceutical drugs flows from the customer or patient through the pharmacy back to the manufacturer. This happens as an iterative process until the patient has his or her prescribed medicine.

In the large pharmacy retail chains such as Walmart, CVS, Walgreens, etc., the procurement of pharmaceutical drugs is typically governed by a master procurement or purchasing agreement in conjunction with a wholesale distributor and the manufacturer. The buyer for a large pharmacy retail chain executes a purchase order on behalf of its stores to the wholesale distributor. The wholesale distributor fulfills the order and issues a debit memo to the pharmacy retail chain. Upon receipt of the ordered pharmaceutical drugs, the pharmacy retail chain's buyer then issues a credit memo back to the wholesale distributor. When the two are reconciled, the actual payment is made as specified by the master procurement agreement.

The process is virtually duplicated between the wholesale distributor and the manufacturer. The procurement of pharmaceutical drugs by a wholesale distributor (i.e., McKesson, AmerisourceBergen, Cardinal, etc.) is typically governed by a master procurement or purchasing agreement in conjunction with a pharmacy retail chain and the manufacturer. The buyer for a wholesale distributor executes a purchase order on behalf of its distribution centers to the manufacturer. The manufacturer fulfills the order and issues a debit memo to the wholesale distributor. Upon receipt of the ordered pharmaceutical drugs, the wholesale distributor's buyer then issues a credit memo back to the manufacturer. When the two are reconciled, the actual payment is made as specified by the master procurement agreement (see Figure 7.1).

In reverse logistics, the complete opposite happens (on paper at least). The pharmacy retail store sends the pharmaceutical drugs back to the manufacturer through the wholesale distributor and issues a debit memo. Upon receipt of the pharmaceutical drugs being returned, the manufacturer issues a credit memo back to the pharmacy retail chain through the wholesale distributor. In the real world of pharmaceuticals, the manufacturer issues the credit memo per a predefined return goods policy. The manufacturers apply these policies at a range of levels. They can include all-encompassing policies that apply to the entire product line they market, drug-specific policies, or of course, purchaser-specific policies that are included as a portion of the procurement agreement on the forward end of the supply chain (see Figure 7.2).

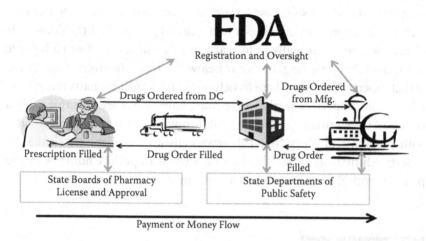

FIGURE 7.1
Pharmaceutical supply chain process, simple forward view.

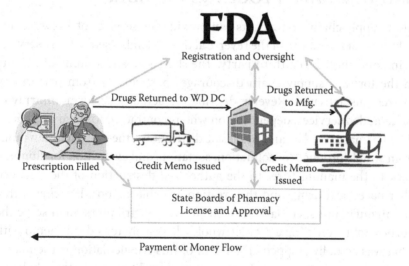

FIGURE 7.2
Pharmaceutical supply chain process, simple reverse logistics view.

THE HUMAN FACTOR

As mentioned before, people make, transport, distribute, dispense, and consume pharmaceutical drugs. People also make mistakes. One of my favorite groups of commercials is the Liberty Mutual "human" commercials, which showcase a series of events when people are not perfect. For example, a man drives into his closed garage door thinking he is in reverse gear but is really in forward; another man cuts down a big tree limb, crunching his neighbor's car below the tree. The overriding theme is that Liberty Mutual is there to help when imperfect humans make mistakes in an imperfect world.[2] (We must have seen these commercials a couple of dozen times, yet they are still funny—and the message resonates with us each and every time.) Reverse logistics providers are similar to Liberty Mutual—they are there to help when imperfect humans in the pharmaceutical drug supply chain make mistakes.

ENTER STAGE RIGHT: REVERSE DISTRIBUTORS AND THIRD-PARTY LOGISTICS PROVIDERS

Most supply chain participants can provide the services of a reverse distributor, but the nature of the reverse activities lends itself to these services being outsourced to a third party. The sheer size and volume of activity in the forward supply chain discourages participants from performing the returns activities. Reverse distributors actually perform an array of value-added services, depending on who is contracted to them as a client. For pharmacy retailers and wholesale distributors, these services can range from simple product consolidation, sortation, and evaluation for shipping back to the manufacturer to the authorized destruction of the returned pharmaceutical drugs and the creation of debit memos. For clients that are manufacturers, comarketers, etc., reverse distributors often serve the purpose of reconciling a retailer/wholesale distributor's debit memo with what was actually shipped. The result of this reconciliation is the manufacturer or the reverse distributor issuing a credit memo to the wholesale distributor (see Figure 7.3).

WHY DO REVERSE DISTRIBUTORS EXIST?

While government regulators and activist clinicians might have you believe that excess supply is not a problem, the reality in the United States is that billions of dollars of "unsalable" pharmaceutical drugs become nothing more

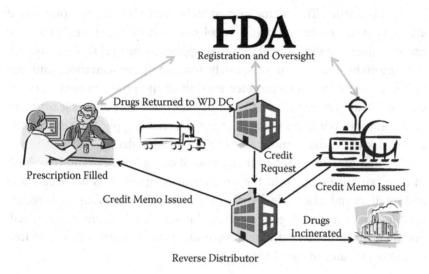

FIGURE 7.3
Pharmaceutical supply chain process, real world reverse logistics view.

than ash at the bottom of an incinerator. One of the main reasons for this is simple. Pharmacy retailers (in conjunction with their wholesale distributors) do not want to stock out of the most popular and profitable pharmaceutical drugs. For example, if someone suffering from strep throat goes to CVS to fulfill his or her prescription for amoxicillin, and CVS cannot fill the prescription for 24 to 48 hours, the patient can and will go to the Walgreens or Walmart pharmacy across the street. He or she may not return to CVS for a long time. Imagine if this were life-sustaining medication such as insulin, or levothyroxine? Pharmacy retailers would rather prevent stock-outs and save customers (and lean on wholesale distributors for expedited service) than minimize inventories and potentially lose customers.

Sometimes there is a valid business and social reason for the excess pharmaceutical drugs. Supply chains for certain drugs can be very long indeed. For instance, it takes six months and 1.2 billion eggs to incubate influenza viruses to use in H1N1 vaccines.[3] Forecast high, and pharmaceutical companies will more than likely be sending a lot of vaccine to reverse distributors. Forecast low, and shortages will be occurring around the country and the lives of people may be at risk. In addition, the U.S. government (and the Centers for Disease Control, among others) gets involved with the forecasting and procurement of H1N1 vaccines.

Similar situations exist in the U.S. hospital environment as well. Imagine a scenario where a patient is admitted to the ER for anaphylactic shock due to a bee sting. The doctor immediately recognizes the symptoms and attempts to administer a shot of epinephrine. What if the epinephrine were not available? The same social incentive applies to medical facilities as well.

As humans, we cannot adequately forecast these scenarios, and our best social response is to produce enough of the products necessary for demand to always be met. In this imperfect world this always leads to an excess supply. With the passage of time, excess supply transforms into excess risk as the drugs move past their expiration date.

Most manufacturers accept it as a cost of doing business and have built in a certain allowance into the procurement agreements between them and retailers and wholesale distributors. When the excess supply is reconciled against the return goods policy, the debit/credit memos are issued, and then the intended path for the product is to be destroyed. We go into this in depth later in the chapter.

THE DRUG QUALITY AND SECURITY ACT: BACK TO THIRD-PARTY LOGISTICS PROVIDERS

As we discussed in Chapter 6, under Title II of the Drug Quality and Security Act, all third-party logistics providers (3PLs) must have a valid state or federal license or licenses and be in full compliance with all reporting requirements. They are considered authorized before federal licensing regulations are effective, unless the FDA makes certain findings and gives notice. By November 27, 2015 (or the second anniversary of the signing of H.R. 3204 into law), the FDA is required to develop new federal standards for licensing of 3PLs and a federal system for 3PL licensing for use when a state system does not meet federal standards. Beginning November 27, 2014, 3PLs must report their licensing status and contact information to the FDA. As of January 1, 2015, all trading partners in the pharmaceutical drug supply chain must be authorized.[4]

The FDA defines 3PLs as "an entity that provides or coordinates warehousing, or other logistics services of a product in interstate commerce on behalf of a manufacturer, wholesale distributor, or dispenser of a product, but does not take ownership of the product, nor have responsibility to direct the sale or disposition of the product.[5]

Casually we telephoned three 3PLs that handle pharmaceutical drugs to find out if they were licensed by their respective states. The answer was yes, they were licensed to do business in their respective states. When we refined our questioning to ask if they were licensed by their respective departments of public safety in the states they distribute pharmaceutical drugs, we were shocked to find out the real answers. In all three cases, the answers were some version of "no, but we are within compliance of state commerce regulations." At least on the surface, it appears that the Drug Quality and Security Act is attempting to close a regulatory loophole by requiring 3PLs to meet minimum federal regulations when handling pharmaceutical drugs. This is especially appropriate when we consider illegal Internet pharmacies and how they distribute their products in the United States through 3PLs.

It is a big step forward to distinguish 3PLs from wholesale distributors, and to require 3PLs to meet federal standards. Why is the new Drug Quality and Security Act so vague regarding reverse distributors? As we can see, they are an important part of the pharmaceutical drug supply chain and very important to protect the quality and secure the supply chain.

REVERSE DISTRIBUTORS

Most pharmaceutical drug manufacturers have a returns allowance for their pharmaceutical drug products. These allowances can vary by pharmaceutical drug, but a rule of thumb is that these allowances are approximately 2.5% of the store or pharmacy value of the drugs. No matter how you cut the numbers, the total dollar amount of these returns is in the tens of billions.

There are three main reverse distributor companies in the marketplace: GENCO, Inmar, and Stericycle. Just like the big three wholesale distributors, these three reverse distributors have rich histories.

Hyman Shear started GENCO in 1898 as H. Shear Trucking Company, delivering commodities in the greater Pittsburgh area, and 117 years later, it is still based in Pittsburgh. Over the years, GENCO evolved from transportation to warehousing as Sam Shear became the CEO in the 1940s. Herb Shear became CEO in 1971 and led the transformation into the GENCO of today. Herb identified unmet needs in the supply chain and launched new services at GENCO, including reverse logistics and later liquidation. Reverse logistics was born of necessity. Oftentimes, returned products would pile up in a distribution center until space became an issue, and then they were sent to a landfill. Herb knew there was still value in the product and pioneered a new software platform called R-Log that manages the complexity of returned product and various disposition channels. Liquidation was the logical next step in reverse logistics as a service to retailers that needed a way to sell returned product. GENCO introduced that service in 1992.[6]

GENCO's health care logistics business entry into reverse logistics was in 2005, when GENCO acquired Capital Returns in Milwaukee, Wisconsin. Capital Returns specialized in receiving expired or recalled pharmaceutical and health care products in a high-security, DEA-approved facility. GENCO leverages its reverse logistics expertise with its knowledge in the health care industry to provide a best-in-class service to pharmaceutical retailers and manufacturers throughout the United States. Today, GENCO is the leader in Product Lifecycle Logistics', which capitalizes on the interconnectedness of the supply chain as warehousing, fulfillment, value-added services, reverse logistics, remarketing, systems, and transportation are maximized. GENCO leverages its supply chain expertise in the health care, technology, consumer and industrial, and retail industries.[7]

Inmar was started in 1981 by John Whitaker as Carolina Coupon Clearing, a business for clearing coupons for retailers. The business expanded into logistics in 1985 with Carolina Reclamation Services. In 1996, Carolina Reclamation Services acquired National Distribution Services and became Carolina Logistics Services (CLS). In 2003, CLS bought Med-Turn, a reverse logistics provider to the pharmaceutical drug industry. In 2005, Carolina Logistics Services bought USF Processors, a leader in reverse logistics in the pharmaceutical drug industry, and merged it with Med-Turn. The new entity was called CLS Med-Turn until 2009, when all entities owned by Inmar were rebranded as Inmar.[8]

Currently, Inmar is a leading provider of technology-driven pharmacy returns management and third-party pharmacy management solutions for more than 24,000 retail pharmacies plus manufacturers, wholesalers, and health systems. Inmar handles pharmaceutical returns from pharmacies, hospitals, medical centers, and wholesale distributors to the destruction site or incinerator. Included in its returns services are the claims and payment reconciliation services for the retail pharmacies and wholesale distributors for reimbursement by the pharmaceutical manufacturers. Inmar processes over 27 million returns annually.[9]

GENCO and Inmar both started through logistics services and grew into becoming reverse distributors in the pharmaceutical drug industry. A third company, Stericycle, was founded in 1989 when the issue of medical waste became national news and the Medical Waster Tracking

Act of 1988 was signed into law. Through acquisitions (notably the Waste Management Medical Waste business in 1996), Stericycle became a leader in the disposal of medical waste and other biohazards. Through the acquisition of DirectRETURN in 2003, Stericycle expanded into recalls and returns. Today Stericycle offers returns services for retail pharmacies, wholesale distributors, and manufacturers that include compliant destruction of all products, from OTC pharmaceutical drug products to controlled substances.[10]

THE PHYSICAL PROCESS OF RETURNS*

Pharmaceutical returns generally fall into one of three categories: saleable, unsaleable, and recalled. The descriptions are somewhat self-explanatory. Saleable returns are products that generally have shelf life remaining and the actual medicine has remained in its original packing. Pharmaceuticals are deemed unsaleable in a similar but opposite manner, including damaged in transit. Product in this condition does not have any shelf life remaining (or not enough to generate a sale), or the actual medicine or therapy has been opened. Recalled pharmaceuticals are products the manufacturer, packager, or FDA has decided should be withdrawn from the market. Technically speaking, recalled products are also unsaleable—which is a reason they are handled so well by the major reverse distributors.

While the three large distributors market themselves as handling all three types of returns, they are three distinct activities with different focuses. This alone creates some differentiation between the services that are provided between GENCO, Inmar, and Stericycle.

Saleable Returns

Saleable returns allow the pharmacy, retailer, or wholesale distributor the opportunity to either find another market in which to sell the product, or to receive full credit for the product because a new market cannot be found due to packaging, labeling, or other reasons. There is a security risk

---

* The following is a synopsis of the physical process of returns. It is a generic summary of our collective experiences of working for, working with, and visiting returns distributors across the country. It must be noted that every return may have its own unique nuance.

with saleable returns, but because they are still considered viable product. Once the pharmacy returns a saleable product back to its wholesale distributor, it is at risk of being stolen and reintroduced into the forward supply chain by someone with the reverse distributor, the courier, or the wholesale distributor. There is a significant financial interest by the owner of the product to protect its supply chain. The burden of saleable returns seems to rest with the wholesale distributor. More than likely, a saleable return will take up residence in a reverse distributor's warehouse, age past its expiration date, and become unsaleable.

Unsaleable Returns

The larger impact the DQSA will have on pharmaceutical returns is for those deemed unsaleable, either by policy or by recall. This is the bread and butter of the work done/performed by the reverse distributors. Let's review the returns process in depth.

The returns process starts when the pharmacist logs on to the web portal of his or her returns company. The pharmacist prints a label, places the product in a returns tote or box, seals the tote or box, and waits for it to be picked up by a wholesale distributor or courier. Some pharmacies still use the U.S. Postal Service (USPS) to ship the returned product because it is usually the lowest-cost alternative.

When the wholesale distributor or courier delivers the product return to the reverse distributor, the reverse distributor merely acknowledges receipt of the tote or box. For the most part, the contents of the tote or box are not reconciled with what the pharmacy believes it may have sent. This is one of the largest risk areas in the returns process. The reverse distributors do check the tote or box for visible damage or signs of tampering upon receipt of the shipment. Since there is a gap of time between receipt of the tote or box and the reconciliation process with the contents, there exists limited visibility to what is happening to the product being returned. This gap of time can be minutes or hours. If we take into account the time from the pharmacist logging on to the web portal to then placing the returned product in the tote or box, the gap may be as long as a day or two.

Upon processing, the contents of the tote or box are reconciled with the pharmacy's shipping information. When processed, the product is identified, quantified, and its condition verified according to the manufacturer's return policy. The reverse distributor at this point aggregates all the data for all the returns for the retail or wholesale distributor client and creates a debit memo, sometimes referred to as an invoice.

Disposition on the retail side of things is determined at this point. If the product is eligible to be returned for credit, either by policy or by law, then the product will be shipped back to the manufacturer or the manufacturer's contracted reverse distributor. When this debit memo is issued, the product becomes the legal property of the manufacturer.

The concept of shipping, though, at this point is a misnomer. First, if the manufacturer's contracted reverse distributor is one and the same as the retailer's or wholesale distributer's, then the product will simply be held for a period of time in case the manufacturer requests a second review. Some manufacturers authorize immediate destruction and credit based on the data provided by the reverse distributor. Others will authorize destruction when they issue the retailer or wholesaler a credit memo.

For product that actually needs to be shipped, there still exists one other possibility. Many times, the manufacturer requires that authorization be given in order to ship the product. When this happens, the product is packaged up and simply waits for the authorization to ship. On certain occasions the manufacturer may never respond to the authorization request or simply issue the credit memo and authorize the product's destruction.

Then there is the case when product actually ships. For the largest manufacturers, the product will merely ship to another reverse distributor. Some specialty pharmaceutical companies still handle their returns in-house. In either case, the product is packed up and, depending on the quantity of inventory being returned, is shipped either parcel or, in cases where the product is not schedule II–controlled substances, by a less-than-truckload (LTL) carrier.

When the product arrives at the manufacturer or its agent, it's again received and processed against the manufacturer's returns policy. After the return is processed, a credit memo is issued against the debit memo. Once this happens, the product is then destroyed.

In all reality, the role of the reverse distributor for retailers and wholesalers is a luxury as an outsourced 3PL. Many pharmacies, and indeed some retailers, often create their own debit memos and just ship product directly to the manufacturer, preferring to be at the mercy of either the manufacturer or the manufacturer's contracted reverse distributor.

With unsaleable product, the absolute science of whether or not the medicine, therapy, or drug is safe and effective may or may not align with legislation, case law, and corporate policies. Antibiotics past their expiration date may still be effective and not pose a substantial risk to those who might consume them. However, in the legitimate channels, these items have been deemed by law to no longer have any value able to be derived from their intended production purpose.

The black market might have other ideas. Reverse distributors have no incentive to engage in reintroducing product into legitimate channels, or illicit channels in the case of controlled substances. The big three reverse distributors have built their businesses over several years and decades, accomplishments that cannot be achieved without integrity and proper operational controls. However, given the low-margin nature of the industry, there is an incentive for individuals (the 1%) to bypass and divert product away from the destruction stream. We believe the biggest risk for diversion and theft is at the linkage points—from the pharmacy to or through the wholesale distributor or courier to the reverse distributor.

TITLE II AND THE VALUE OF RETURNS

We believe the question that the CEO, and especially the CFO, of pharmaceutical drug manufacturers should be asking is, "How might we reduce the cost of our returns from 2.5% to 2.0%?" This would produce a half point of margin for the company, less any initial costs, but plus any operational efficiencies that result from the effort.

As we described earlier, pharmaceutical drug returns primarily occur because of recalls, expiring drugs, product damage in transit, and product to be quarantined (i.e., illegitimate product). With the new Title II track and trace regulations, we believe that the time has come for someone innovative to unlock the latent value of returns.

The returns process described earlier focuses on the operational process and the issuing of debit and credit memos. The value today for multiple parties is perceived to be twofold: to minimize the cost to return and destroy the drugs, and to speed up the issuance of credit memos from the appropriate parties. The value tomorrow goes far beyond the value today.

With the advent of product identifiers enabling product tracing on all pharmaceutical drug packaging, reverse distributors and wholesale distributors can now work toward the answer to the question, why does this return exist? When the retail pharmacy sends pharmaceutical drugs back to the wholesale distributor, it wants it done swiftly and with financial accuracy. We discussed in Chapter 5 that physical space in a pharmacy is at a premium, and any pharmaceutical drug that is unsaleable or unusable to the pharmacy is considered a liability.

The wholesale distributor may receive perfectly good product well within its code date. This product can be either placed back into inventory or sent to a reverse distributor. Either way, pharmaceutical drugs being sent back by the pharmacy that represent good product potentially means a breakdown in the forecasting or ordering processes of the forward supply chain. We mentioned that it is common for the forward supply chain to overorder to avoid any stock-outs of "must have" medications. However, we know that for certain drug categories the overproduction/supply is significant. It is easier for the pharmacy to accept the better code date product and return the older product, even though the current product may have weeks or even months of shelf life left.

There are three primary ways to address the oversupply of these product groups. The first one is to perform a returns analysis by product group by pharmacy. This will identify specific pharmacies that may be the biggest offenders. The second one is to roll up the returns by product group, and to adjust the procurement and manufacturing processes to produce closer to the level of demand. The naysayers in pharmaceutical drug manufacturing will of course say that any shrinkage in supply will produce stockouts. Manufacturing executives are also quick to point out the value of leveraging fixed assets to lower the cost of each drug unit manufactured. This sounds logical, but some department is picking up the cost of returns. We have already identified a couple of supply chain software providers that can match supply with demand in near real time and shift the supply to avoid these situations. In addition, excess supply does absorb resources to the warehouse, transporting, handling, and destroying it.

The third way is for wholesale distributors to expand their same-day service when a shortage of critical drugs occurs and next-day service for not so critical drugs.

Product damaged in transit is also an area that can be tracked through the product identifiers. There are numerous reasons that product is damaged in transit. With the right analysis, we believe that the reasons for the damage can be determined and corrective action taken to prevent the damage. This all sounds logical and doable today. What has inhibited the process to realize this value? Let's take a quick look at the inhibitors.

Another consideration is to understand the true market value of the product returned. The sale price (the credit amount) includes full recovery of the R&D and advertisement, etc., to produce the drug. As evidenced by the change in price once a drug goes generic, the price, including R&D, is very different than the actual cost of the drug, which may be destroyed. This also reinforces the belief that the pharmaceutical drug returns business is really a finance-driven business, enabled by a logistics-driven activity.

WHAT ARE THE CRITICAL INHIBITORS?

Organizational Levels Involved

To make the adjustments to supply to meet the demand and reduce inventory in the supply chain, the executives (C-suite) must be involved. This especially means the office of the chief financial officer (CFO), where the profits and losses (P&Ls), balance sheet, and sources and uses of funds for the pharmaceutical drug company come together. Currently, the reverse distributors and the wholesale distributors work with low to, at most, middle management personnel managing returns for the pharmaceutical drug companies. At the low and middle management levels, the personnel work primarily with an expense budget. Their focus is to manage returns down to under the target level (identified earlier as approximately 2.5%). We have seen instances where their approval of returns (and payment for the returns) is held over month to month to make sure their targets are met. We think this is wasteful, because it only adds cost through additional storage and sometimes handling charges.

Availability and Access to Relevant Data

The why behind returns resides in a few specific areas of the pharmaceutical supply chain. The pharmacist has the best knowledge of the reason(s) for the return. When he or she logs on to the web portal of the reverse distributor (or in some cases, the wholesale distributor), the reason code should be keyed in for all returns. The wholesale distributors will be in the center for most, but not all, returns. Usually they have a good view of the why behind returns. The reverse distributor will have the second-best knowledge of the why behind unsaleable returns after the pharmacist. This includes saleable returns that go to an aging graveyard to become unsaleable returns. As our readers can see, the pharmaceutical drug companies are absent from this information flow until the application for returns credit is made. By this time, the reasons behind the returns are genericized and aggregated, so meaningful data are limited to the pharmaceutical drug companies. A couple of reverse distributors sell raw data to pharmaceutical drug companies, but the conversion from data to information to relevant knowledge on what it all means to the C-suite executives appears to be missing with several companies.

Incentives

Right now the incentive with reverse distributors and wholesale distributors is to increase, not decrease, the volume of returns and try to expedite payment from the pharmaceutical drug manufacturers for the returns. The only exception we can find is the storage charges assessed for returns, which are barely compensatory for the space the returns utilize. We asked a couple of wholesale distributors about this concept. We heard one manager at a wholesale distributor say, "Why do we want to ever reduce the volume of returns? We make money on returns." Enough said!

SUMMARY

Reverse logistics is defined as the supply chain in reverse. Returns occur because of excess supply or saleable returns, unsaleable returns, and recalled product. The companies that handle returns are called reverse distributors. The big three reverse distributors are GENCO, Inmar, and Stericycle. These three companies have rich histories and offer a wide variety of services to the pharmaceutical drug manufacturers, wholesale distributors, and pharmacies. Title II of the Drug Quality and Security Act, through its mandated product identifiers and product tracking, will provide an opportunity to track and trace pharmaceutical drugs to and from the pharmacy to reverse distributors, enhancing the ability to determine the why behind returns. There is a real opportunity for pharmaceutical drug companies to reduce their overall returns cost by avoiding the returns through adjustments in their forward supply chains. Sometimes, there are unintended benefits from new regulations, not just unintended consequences.

ENDNOTES

1. John Paine, Things That Go Bump in the Night, Veracity, 2013, http://sharedveracity. net/2013/05/04/things-that-go-bump-in-the-night/.
2. http://www.libertymutual.com/liberty-mutual-videos/commercials.
3. How the H1N1 Vaccine Is Made, Kotteke.org, http://kottke.org/09/11/how-the-h1n1-vaccine-is-made.
4. Connie Jung and Eleni Anagnostiadis, Drug Supply Chain Security Act, Federal–State Collaboration, FDA, 2014, pp. 14, 18, http://www.nabp.net/system/rich/rich_files/rich_files/000/000/385/original/dscsafederalstatecollaboration-final.pdf.
5. Ibid., p. 35.
6. http://www.genco.com/About/history.php.
7. Ibid.; Ryan Kelly, Senior VP Strategy and Marketing, GENCO, November 8, 2014.
8. https://www.inmar.com/Pages/About_Us/Inmar-History.aspx.
9. https://www.inmar.com/Pages/Healthcare-Network/default.aspx.
10. http://www.stericycle.com/history.

8

---

*All Those "Lettered"
Government Agencies*

![separator]

OVERVIEW

My regional pharmacy manager contact told me that there are so many
government agencies responsible for overseeing the manufacturing, transportation and warehousing, and distribution and dispensing of pharmaceutical drugs, it reminds her of the 1951 Abbott and Costello routine
"Who's on First?" (I was not born yet, but if you have not watched this
routine, I have provided a link to it.[1]) Both the routine and sorting out the
agencies in charge are very confusing, to say the least. In this chapter, I try
to give an overview of each agency and how the agency is tasked to enforce
the Drug Quality and Security Act.

THE FEDERAL AND STATE BOYS AND GIRLS

The primary federal agencies responsible for overseeing the manufacturing, transportation and warehousing, and distribution and dispensing of
pharmaceutical drugs are the U.S. Food and Drug Administration (FDA)
and the U.S. Drug Enforcement Administration (DEA). The primary state
agencies are the state boards of pharmacy, the state departments of public
safety, and the state medical boards. Let's start with the FDA.

U.S. Food and Drug Administration

Several of the compounding pharmacy owners I interviewed complained about selected FDA inspectors. When I questioned why, there were three reasons for these complaints. The first reason was not the inspector, but a lack of structured audit criteria that produced a standard audit template. We discussed a private sector alternative to this in Chapter 3. The second reason was a distaste for the added regulations. Again, this is not an inspector issue. From what I can tell at this point, the FDA inspectors are focused on defining compounding pharmacies that compound to specific patient prescriptions, and then assume all other compounding pharmacies are compound manufacturers (and subject to current good manufacturing practices (cGMP), etc.). I do know of one FDA inspector that found one example "in the gray area" and deferred the determination of the compounding pharmacy to the state board of pharmacy. However, this appears to be an exception rather than the rule. The third reason was the auditor himself or herself. I will attribute this to the 1% we have been discussing since my introduction. There are jerks and bad people in every profession. However, what I have found during my book research is that the FDA has outstanding professionals trying to do their best given their task to protect the public from unsafe pharmaceutical drugs. The following is a history of the FDA, dedicated to the 99% of these FDA professionals.

The FDA* has a long and proud history. Despite all the wrongdoing or alleged wrongdoing in the Internal Revenue Service (IRS) and other government agencies, we should be thankful that we have a strong FDA and dedicated workers who make up the agency. I have traveled all around the world and lived in South America, and from my perspective, we have the best consumer protection as it relates to food, drugs, cosmetics, and other products.

Officially, the FDA as a law enforcement agency dates back to 1906 and the 1906 Food and Drug Act. However, as an institution, scientific activity in food and other agricultural substances to protect consumers dates back to 1862. Federal concern for drugs started with the establishment of U.S. Customs laboratories to administer the Import Drugs Act of 1848. This act was established to counteract counterfeit, contaminated, diluted, and decomposed drug materials (sound familiar?).[2]

---

* The following was largely excerpted from an article on the FDA website titled "The Story of the Laws behind the Labels" by Wallace F. Janssen, FDA historian. It is provided with approval from the FDA.

Troubling Marketplace

Wallace Janssen writes about how bad conditions were in the U.S. food and drug industries a century ago. The use of chemical preservatives, primitive sanitation, the lack of refrigeration capabilities beyond the use of ice, the lack of bacteriology discoveries, and other factors combined for very poor and dangerous conditions. Medicines containing such drugs as opium, morphine, heroin, and cocaine were sold without restriction. Labeling gave no hint of their presence.[3]

We need to be thankful to live in the United States. I have been to third world countries, and to an extent, some of these conditions still exist today. We have to look no further than Central and South America to find countries where clean drinking water is scarce and refrigeration is at a premium outside the major cities. The same holds true in India, China, and Southeast Asia. This is why we need to be vigilant on imports, especially in terms of food and pharmaceutical drugs.

The 1906 Pure Food and Drug Act (The Wiley Act)

It took 27 years to pass the 1906 Pure Food and Drug Act, commonly referred to as the Wiley Act. Dr. Harvey Washington Wiley is credited as being the main crusader for the passage of this act. Wiley believed, among other things, that the burden of proving food and drug safety should fall on the producer, and that no chemicals should be used without informing the consumer on the label—basic principles of today's law and regulations. Ingredients in the drugs were also of high concern. For the first time, ingredients such as alcohol, morphine, opium, and cannabis had to be listed on labels.[4] He worked hard with other chemists to pursue passage of this important act (Figure 8.1). (See Chapter 10 for more information on Dr. Wiley.)

The Wiley Act of 1906 was signed by President Theodore Roosevelt, becoming the first federal law regulating foods and drugs. The effective date of the act, June 30, 1906, is considered the founding date for the FDA.[5] This law also defined *misbranding* and *adulteration* for the first time. It also prescribed penalties for each offense. The law recognized the U.S. Pharmacopeia and the National Formulary as standards authorities for drugs.[6]

Enforcing the Wiley Act

Administration of the new law was assigned to the Bureau of Chemistry. Through reorganization, the Food, Drug, and Insecticide Administration

FIGURE 8.1
Association of Official Agricultural Chemists, 1887. (From FDA. With permission.)

was formed in 1927, to be renamed in 1930 as the Food and Drug Administration (FDA). In 1940, the FDA was transferred from the U.S. Department of Agriculture to the Federal Security Agency. In 1953, the Federal Security Agency became the Department of Health, Education, and Welfare—now the Department of Health and Human Services.[7]

The Federal Food, Drug, and Cosmetic Act

In 1938, the U.S. Congress passed the Federal Food, Drug, and Cosmetic Act (FFDCA), giving the FDA the authority to oversee the safety of food, drugs, medical devices, and cosmetics. On June 25, 1938, President Roosevelt signed the Federal Food, Drug, and Cosmetic Act. The FFDCA replaced the Wiley Act.[8]

Wallace Janssen identified a number of improvements with the FFDCA versus the Wiley Act. These were as follows:

- Drug manufacturers were required to provide scientific proof that new products could be safely used before putting them on the market.
- Cosmetics and therapeutic devices were regulated for the first time.
- Proof of fraud was no longer required to stop false claims for drugs.
- Addition of poisonous substances to foods was prohibited except where unavoidable or required in production. Safe tolerances were authorized for residues of such substances, for example, pesticides.

FIGURE 8.2
An FDA analyst certifying penicillin samples. (From FDA. With permission.)

- Specific authority was provided for factory inspections.
- Food standards were required to be set up when needed "to promote honesty and fair dealing in the interest of consumers."
- Federal court injunctions against violations were added to the previous legal remedies of product seizures and criminal prosecutions.[9]

The Preventive Amendments

During my introduction, I mentioned the correlation between longevity and the advancement of pharmaceutical drugs from 1930 through the present time. Wallace Janssen cites the FDDCA of 1938, World War II and wartime demands, and the development of new "wonder drugs," especially antibiotics, for setting the table for what he calls the preventative amendments. These new wonder drugs were made subject to FDA testing beginning with insulin in 1941, followed by amendments addressing penicillin and other antibiotics beginning in 1945 (Figure 8.2).[10]

The 1962 Kefauver–Harris Amendment

The 1962 Kefauver–Harris Amendment was an amendment to the FDDCA of 1938. This was an important act because it required drug manufacturers

FIGURE 8.3
President Kennedy signing the 1962 Drug Amendments. (From FDA. With permission.)

to provide proof of the effectiveness as well as safety of drugs (called proof of efficacy) before FDA approval. The nature of the evidence for effectiveness had to be much more rigorous, and developed by those qualified to do so. The FDA was given greater oversight of clinical investigations, and patients involved in drug experiments had to supply informed consent that they were subjects in a drug study. In addition, this amendment required drug advertising to disclose accurate information about side effects and efficacy of treatments. The law gave greater authority to FDA inspectors to access certain drug manufacturing records, and it instituted systematic good manufacturing practices. The amendment was a response to the thalidomide tragedy, in which thousands of children were born with birth defects as a result of their mothers taking thalidomide for morning sickness during pregnancy. The law was signed by President John F. Kennedy on October 10, 1962 (Figure 8.3).[11]

Wallace Janssen did a marvelous job detailing the history of the FDA. His article, complete with pictures of key figures throughout the FDA's history, can be found on the FDA website. His article was published in the *FDA Consumer* in June 1981. One of his main observations is that the FDA's laws have changed from being primarily criminal statutes, protecting consumers through the deterrent effect of court proceedings, to laws that are now dominantly preventive through informative regulations and controls before marketing. In my opinion, someone needs to build on this history and detail the fine work of the FDA from 1981 through the passing of the Drug Quality and Safety Act of 2013. The following are a couple of key acts that have been signed into law since 1981.

The 1988 Food and Drug Administration Act

The 1988 Food and Drug Administration Act officially established the FDA as an agency of the Department of Health and Human Services with a commissioner of food and drugs appointed by the president with the advice and consent of the Senate. This act identified the responsibilities of the HHS secretary and the commissioner for research, enforcement, education, and information.[12]

The Prescription Drug Marketing Act of 1988

The Prescription Drug Marketing Act of 1988 bans the diversion of prescription drugs from legitimate commercial channels. The new law requires drug wholesalers and distributors to be licensed by the states, restricts reimportation from other countries, and bans sale, trade, or purchase of drug samples, and traffic or counterfeiting of redeemable drug coupons.[13]

Food and Drug Administration Modernization Act of 1997

This act reauthorizes the Prescription Drug User Fee Act of 1992 and mandates the most wide-ranging reforms in agency practices since 1938. Provisions include measures to accelerate review of devices, regulate advertising of unapproved uses of approved drugs and devices, and regulate health claims for foods.[14]

FDA Summary

Regarding pharmaceutical drugs, the men and women of the FDA have a very difficult task. They are responsible for protecting the public health by ensuring the safety, security, and efficacy of these drugs. They have also been relied upon for the past 150+ years to use science-based information to promote innovation to help make our pharmaceutical drugs safer, more effective, and more affordable. It is not easy to take a law and flesh out the regulations and details supporting the law, protecting the public health and the industry as a whole. As consumers, most of the FDA employees deserve our thanks for helping secure our availability of needed pharmaceutical drugs. We all hope this performance continues with the rollout of the Drug Quality and Safety Act.

U.S. Drug Enforcement Administration

The DEA is not expressly responsible for the new Drug Quality and Safety Act. It is, however, involved with the safety and security of our controlled substance pharmaceutical drugs. The Title II track and trace regulations, as developed by the FDA, will affect the DEA's operations. In my opinion, they are one of my most admired agencies of the U.S. federal government. Let's take a look at the history of the DEA, its responsibilities and offices/sections, and how Title II will impact its activities.

History: Controlled Substances Act and the DEA

The Controlled Substances Act (CSA) was passed as part of the Comprehensive Drug Abuse Prevention and Control Act of 1970 and signed into law by President Richard Nixon. The CSA is the federal U.S. drug policy under which the manufacture, importation, possession, use, and distribution of certain substances are regulated. The legislation created five schedules (classifications), with varying qualifications for a substance to be included in each. The DEA currently works with the FDA to determine which substances are placed in the five schedules.[15]

The DEA was created by President Richard Nixon through an executive order in July 1973 in order to establish a single unified command to combat "an all-out global war on the drug menace." At its outset, the DEA had 1,470 special agents and a budget of less than $75 million. Today, the DEA has approximately 5,000 special agents and a budget of $2.02 billion.[16]

In my opinion, the number of the DEA special agents is paltry compared to the responsibilities of the agency and the geographic coverage. The DEA has 5,000 special agents to cover 50 states (and international investigations and activities) to combat drug smuggling and use of controlled substances. This means, all things being equal and leaving out its international work, that the DEA has 100 special agents to cover each state. It does share jurisdiction domestically with the Federal Bureau of Investigation (FBI) and Immigration and Customs Enforcement (ICE), but it has sole responsibility for pursuing U.S. drug investigations outside the United States. It seems to me that we need 100 special agents alone to cover El Paso and the criminal activities regarding controlled substances emerging from Ciudad Juarez, let alone all the other hot spots. The mission and responsibilities of the DEA are broad and far-reaching. Let's review what our 5,000 special agents are trying to achieve.

Overview/Mission

The mission of the DEA is to enforce the controlled substances laws and regulations of the United States and bring to the criminal and civil justice systems of the United States, or any other competent jurisdiction, those organizations and principal members of organizations involved in the growing, manufacture, or distribution of controlled substances appearing in or destined for illicit traffic in the United States, and to recommend and support nonenforcement programs aimed at reducing the availability of illicit controlled substances on the domestic and international markets.[17]

Responsibilities

In carrying out its mission as the agency responsible for enforcing the controlled substances laws and regulations of the United States, the DEA's primary responsibilities include the following:

- Investigation and preparation for the prosecution of major violators of controlled substances laws operating at interstate and international levels
- Investigation and preparation for the prosecution of criminals and drug gangs who perpetrate violence in our communities and terrorize citizens through fear and intimidation
- Management of a national drug intelligence program in cooperation with federal, state, local, and foreign officials to collect, analyze, and disseminate strategic and operational drug intelligence information
- Seizure and forfeiture of assets derived from, traceable to, or intended to be used for illicit drug trafficking
- Enforcement of the provisions of the Controlled Substances Act as they pertain to the manufacture, distribution, and dispensing of legally produced controlled substances

- Coordination and cooperation with federal, state, and local law enforcement officials on mutual drug enforcement efforts and enhancement of such efforts through exploitation of potential interstate and international investigations beyond local or limited federal jurisdictions and resources
- Coordination and cooperation with federal, state, and local agencies, and with foreign governments, in programs designed to reduce the availability of illicit abuse-type drugs on the U.S. market through nonenforcement methods such as crop eradication, crop substitution, and training of foreign officials
- Responsibility, under the policy guidance of the secretary of state and U.S. ambassadors, for all programs associated with drug law enforcement counterparts in foreign countries
- Liaison with the United Nations, INTERPOL, and other organizations on matters relating to international drug control programs[18]

Offices/Sections

The DEA has several offices/sections that parallel its responsibilities. These offices/sections include the Administrative Support Section (TRA), the Academic Operations Unit (TRDA), the Clandestine Laboratory Training Unit (TRDC), the Firearms Training Unit (TRDG), the Intelligence Training Section (TRN), the International Law Enforcement Academies (ILEAs), International Mobile Units A, B, and C (TRIA, TRIB, and TRIC), the Leadership and Development Unit (TRDL), Planning and Evaluation Staff (TRP), the Practical Applications Unit (TRDP), the Specialized Training Unit (TRDS), the Tactical Safety and Survival Unit (TRDT), the Legal Instruction Section (CCT), and the Diversion Operations Unit (TRDD).[19]

The DEA Office of Diversion Control

The DEA Office of Diversion Control focuses on drug theft and loss, import and export controls, the controlled substances ordering system, the inventorying and monitoring of all surrendered controlled substances, and the reports required by 21 Code of Federal Regulations (CFR) (destruction of controlled substances, chemical import and export declarations, controlled substances import and export permits, and quota applications for the procurement, import, and manufacturing of controlled substances).[20]

There are literally 14 pages of controlled substances that the DEA must monitor.[21] Earlier in the book, we discussed the fact that a number of controlled substance painkillers have become the drug of choice on street corners. With such a small staff, it is of little wonder why emphasis is placed on the ordering, manufacturing, import and export permitting, and destruction monitoring activities of controlled substances.

The added Title II track and trace regulations from the Drug Quality and Security Act should help the DEA in its activities. This is especially true, given the right technology, for monitoring the movement and inventory locations of controlled substances from point of manufacturer through wholesale distributors to retail pharmacies. The ability to monitor controlled substances will allow special agents to diagnose when and where diversion occurs as controlled substances are discovered in locations they are not supposed to be at the time. It will also help these special agents determine who is responsible when controlled substances are diverted in the supply chain.

In Chapter 6, we discussed the key role the DEA played in shutting down a couple of big-time pill mills in Florida. With a bigger budget, enhanced supply chain real-time tracking technology, and track and trace help from the Drug Quality and Security Act, the DEA could do wonders in minimizing the availability of controlled substances to people without prescriptions from a doctor. This would certainly help minimize the crime associated with buying illegal drugs and, more importantly, minimize the number of overdose deaths associated with controlled substances.

The CBP and the DEA

The Customs and Border Protection (CBP) has the responsibility to keep our borders secure. CBP agents must inspect everyone arriving at a U.S. port of entry. Their initial inspection includes three questions: the person's citizenship, the nature of the person's trip (business or pleasure), and if the person is bringing anything into the United States. The CBP does have the legal authority to inspect baggage, cars, trucks, and airplanes to look for prohibited items, ranging from terrorist weapons to controlled substances.[22]

When I lived in South America for a couple of years, I traveled from multiple South American cities back to the United States through Miami. On every trip, I was met by CBP agents in customs and immigration. They had a host of dogs searching for prohibited items. One time I was randomly selected for a thorough search. The one agent, a man, patted me down while the other agent, a woman, had a female beagle that sniffed all of my belongings. The beagle stayed around me for an extended time, the reason being I had two golden retrievers at the time. Once the woman agent understood I was a dog owner, she moved on to the next traveler. I asked if they ever found anything. The female agent pointed to a holding area with a half-dozen people in handcuffs being guarded by armed agents. She said those are the ones trying to bring in illegal controlled substances. The DEA was called to take control of the controlled substances and start the investigation in preparation to prosecute these offenders. And here I thought they only found Cuban cigars on these flights!

DEA National Prescription Drug Take-Back Day

The DEA works with multiple law enforcement agencies, hospitals, pharmacies, and other entities to accept excess pharmaceutical drugs back from individuals. This is a wonderful service to the general public. According to a 2013 report, an estimated 6.5 million people ages 12 and older are "current nonmedical users of prescription drugs." In addition, an estimated 70% of people who misuse prescription painkillers for the first time have told authorities that they obtained the drugs from friends or relatives, including home medicine cabinets.[23]

"As recently as 2011, more than half of the 41,300 unintentional drug overdose deaths in the United States involved prescription drugs—and opioid pain relievers were involved in nearly 17,000 of those deaths," Attorney General Eric Holder said. In addition, nearly 110 Americans died every day that year from drug overdoses, according to the Centers for Disease Control and Prevention.[24]

The DEA take-back day was September 27, 2014. Prior to 2010 and the initiation of the Pharmaceutical Drug Take-Back Program, people often disposed of leftover or excess medications by flushing them down the toilet or throwing them in the trash. Each of those methods posed potential risks—one to the environment and the other to children who have fished supplies out of the garbage.[25] In addition, it keeps the excess pharmaceutical drugs away from the black market.

DEA Summary

Although the DEA is not directly responsible for establishing the regulations for the Drug Quality and Security Act, it will be affected due to the Title II track and trace regulations for pharmaceutical drugs as they relate to controlled substances. There is a real opportunity for the DEA as it establishes and monitors quota applications for the ordering and procurement, manufacture, import and export permitting, disbursement, and destruction of controlled substances. The opportunity is to utilize real-time supply chain tracking technology to monitor the movement of controlled substances. This way, the DEA will be able to identify the perpetrators of diversion and the illegal disbursement of controlled substances. We should also be grateful to the professionals at the DEA for their service in protecting the public from misuse of controlled substances!

State Boards of Pharmacy

The state boards of pharmacy protect public health through the licensing of pharmacists and their pharmacist competence assessment programs. The basic premise is that pharmacists serve as health care professionals, providing patient care through the patients' medications as prescribed by a licensed physician. It is up to the state regulatory agencies to enforce minimum standards of care.

During my research for this book I worked with five state boards of pharmacy. All five have dedicated professionals that are "all in" to protect public health and ensure the availability of needed pharmaceutical drugs (compounded ones included) to patients in need. They are also all in to protect the public from the abuse of pharmaceutical drugs, and support regulations that make it difficult for the bad guys to get drugs illegally. However, everyone I spoke with is concerned and worried that excess regulations may impede the flow of legal drugs to patients in need and with prescriptions.

State Departments of Public Safety

Once the laws are made by the states and the U.S. Congress, it is up to the enforcement agencies and the states to enforce them. Regarding controlled substances, the DEA has the authority to enforce the controlled substances laws and regulations. However, as we stated, it only has 5,000 special agents to work the 14+ pages of controlled substances. The state law enforcement agencies, largely through the state departments of public safety, augment the DEA in enforcing the controlled substances laws and regulations. They primarily do this by providing personal and financial protection to the citizens in their respective states through the enforcement and education services to regulated businesses (i.e., pharmacies) and individuals (i.e., pharmacists). In addition, state law enforcement agencies partner with the DEA to help the DEA execute its Pharmaceutical Drug Take-Back Day.

The state departments of public safety are very busy. They are known for their efforts in issuing driver's licenses, AMBER alerts, highway patrols, vehicle inspections, and many other activities. However, the two state department of public safety representatives I spoke with both said their efforts with pharmaceutical drugs, and especially controlled substances, are very high priorities. The one in the Northeast told me that the abuse of controlled substances leads to other crimes, from armed robbery to identity theft, to fund the addicts' habits. The one in the Southwest said the abuse of pharmaceutical drugs was directly interrelated with armed robbery, identity theft, prostitution, and especially border security from a supply standpoint.

State Medical Boards

The state medical boards approve and license physicians, physician assistants, acupuncturists, surgical assistants, and physicians-in-training. These state medical boards process the applications of practitioners and nonprofit entities to determine whether they meet all the criteria to practice or operate in their respective states. Applicants must graduate from appropriate educational institutions, pass national exams, pass the appropriate state exam, and possess good professional character. Two state boards that I contacted said they do extensive background checks, and disqualify applicants for felonies and other offenses that demonstrate poor professional character.

This is important, because as we stated earlier in the book, it all starts with a prescription. Physicians prescribe medicines (compounded, controlled substances, and others) that can provide patients needed help or could be deadly if abused or used recreationally. From pill mills to Internet pharmacies, a bad physician can do a lot of damage if he or she misuses the license he or she has from a state medical board.

I know one lady who is a recovering alcoholic and has not had a drink in 30+ years. She has made it her life's work to help other alcoholics. She visits a local hospital weekly, where she counsels doctors and nurses who are alcoholics. Some of the doctors are also drug users. Their habits cost a fortune. These doctors are very vulnerable to misusing their privileges and becoming the doctor of choice for pill mills or illegal users of drugs as a way to fund their own habits.

When I first heard these stories, I was shocked. My friend told me that doctors are people just like you and me, and suffer from the same stresses and illnesses as everyone else. According to the Henry J. Kaiser Family Foundation, in November 2012 there were 397,130 primary care physicians and 437,639 specialist physicians, for a total of 834,769 total physicians in the United States.[26] According to the National Council on Alcohol and Drug Dependence (NCADD), 1 in 12 adults (8.5%) suffer from alcohol abuse or dependence, and 8% have used an illegal drug in the past 30 days.[27] Even if these were the same people, and the percentages applied to physicians, that means we have between 66,782 and 70,955 physicians who suffer from alcohol abuse or dependence or have used an illegal drug in the past 30 days. The more the state medical boards test for fitness or good professional character, the faster these doctors with issues can get help and the safer their patients will be from malpractice. The ones that slip through the cracks will be the ones that the DEA and state departments of public safety will have to catch!

SUMMARY

There are several agencies that are responsible for various aspects of the pharmaceutical drug supply chain. The FDA is responsible for protecting the public health by ensuring the safety, efficacy, and security of human drugs (among other responsibilities). The FDA is also responsible for advancing the public health through accelerating innovations that make medicines more effective, safer, and more affordable. With this mission, the FDA is defining the regulations as required with the Drug Quality and Security Act. The DEA enforces the controlled substances laws and regulations of the United States. In my opinion, the DEA is understaffed and underfunded to enforce these laws, bring the criminals to justice, and perform the preventive tasks as outlined in its stated mission. The state boards of pharmacy regulate pharmacists. The state departments of public safety fill in the gaps at the local level and enforce all federal and state laws regarding the manufacture, transport, warehouse, delivery, and dispensing of pharmaceutical drugs. The state medical boards regulate the doctors writing the prescriptions. This is no trivial task! There are other agencies that may be involved, situation dependent. These agencies include, among others, the FBI, the Consumer Products Safety Commission, and the Environmental Protection Agency (EPA). There is no shortage of lettered agencies involved. One needs a scorecard to determine who's on first!

ENDNOTES

1. https://www.youtube.com/watch?v=EockdNVu8R8.
2. Wallace F. Janssen, The Story of the Laws behind the Labels, *FDA Consumer*, 1981, http://www.fda.gov/AboutFDA/WhatWeDo/History/Overviews/ucm056044.htm.
3. Ibid.
4. Ibid.
5. Ibid.
6. Ibid.
7. Ibid.
8. Michael Klein, FDA Regulatory Processes and Standards for Review and Approval of Opioid Analgesics, FDA, http://www.fda.gov/downloads/drugs/drugsafety/information bydrugclass/ucm163691.pdf; http://www.fda.gov/aboutFDA/WhatWeDo/History/origin/ucm054826.htm.
9. Wallace F. Janssen, The Story of the Laws behind the Labels, *FDA Consumer*, 1981, http://www.fda.gov/AboutFDA/WhatWeDo/History/Overviews/ucm056044.htm.
10. Ibid.
11. 50 Years: The Kefauver–Harris Amendments, FDA, http://www.fda.gov/Drugs/NewsEvents/ucm320924.htm; ibid.
12. Significant Dates in U.S. Food and Drug Law History, FDA, http://www.fda.gov/aboutfda/whatwedo/history/milestones/ucm128305.htm.
13. Ibid.
14. Ibid.
15. Controlled Substance Schedules, Office of Diversion Control, DEA, DOJ, http://www.deadiversion.usdoj.gov/schedules/.
16. DEA History, DEA, http://www.justice.gov/dea/about/history.shtml.
17. Ibid.
18. DEA Mission Statement, DEA, http://www.justice.gov/dea/about/mission.shtml.
19. DEA, http://www.justice.gov/dea/index.shtml.
20. Reports Required by 21 CFR, Office of Diversion Control, DEA, DOJ, http://www.deadiversion.usdoj.gov/21cfr_reports/index.html.
21. Controlled Substances, Office of Diversion Control, DEA, DOJ, http://www.deadiversion.usdoj.gov/schedules/orangebook/c_cs_alpha.pdf.
22. CBP Search Authority, U.S. Customs and Border Protection, https://help.cbp.gov/app/answers/detail/a_id/176/kw/controlled%20substances/session/L3RpbWUvMT QxMDU0MzMwNy9zaWQvY01RUExkMm0%3D.
23. Kevin Johnson, Opioids Are High on the List in Rx Drug-Return Effort, *USA Today*, 2014, http://www.usatoday.com/story/news/nation/2014/09/08/hospitals-pharmacies-to-accept-excess-prescription-pills/15275559/.
24. Ibid.

25. Ibid.
26. Total Professionally Active Physicians, State Health Facts, KFF, http://kff.org/other/state-indicator/total-active-physicians/.
27. Alcohol & Drug Information, NCADD, https://ncadd.org/for-the-media/alcohol-a-drug-information.

9

Pulling It All Together: Public Policy and Other Items of Note

OVERVIEW

In Chapters 1 through 8, we covered the Drug Quality and Security Act and its impact on the primary supply chain participants. There are other participants and areas of interest that are impacted as well. In this chapter, I cover a few of these items prior to my overall summary.

PUBLIC POLICY

Public policy is defined by the *Merriam-Webster Dictionary* as follows:

1. The governing policy within a community as embodied in its legislative and judicial enactments which serve as a basis for determining what acts are to be regarded as contrary to the public good
2. The principle of law by virtue of which acts contrary to the public good are held invalid[1]

Regarding the Drug Quality and Security Act, public policy worked, but I do have a nagging question: What took our lawmakers so long? The answer may be in why our drug laws in the past 100 years were passed by Congress.

The Pure Food and Drug Act of 1906, or the Wiley Act, took 27 years to pass and become law. During this time, thousands of people were taking medicines (unknowingly and unintentionally) with high alcohol content, infant syrups with opium, and some medicines with poison. It must be noted that the therapeutic claims for many medicines were unlimited and unbridled. Also during this time, the science of chemistry was advancing significantly. Congress acted when the science identified what was actually happening with the medicines and qualified the therapeutic claims. The 1938 Federal Food, Drug, and Cosmetics Act was passed after 100+ people died who took a sulfanilamide medication where diethyleneglycol was used to dissolve the medicine into a liquid. The Kefauver–Harris Amendment of 1962 was passed after thousands of babies were born in Europe and elsewhere with shortened, missing, or flipper-like arms and legs to mothers that took thalidomide for morning sickness. As we mentioned throughout the book, the Drug Quality and Security Act was passed after 64 people died and 750 people were infected with fungal meningitis from tainted medicine from the New England Compounding Center (NECC) (Figure 9.1).[2] *Why does it seem to take people dying for public policy to take hold in our country?*

One answer is certainly politics and the fundamental differences between Republicans and Democrats. The Republicans believe in less government regulation and the free market, while Democrats believe in more government regulation and a regulated marketplace. The pendulum between the two is constantly swinging, and the answer is always somewhere in the middle. To crack the barriers of each party, it usually takes a calamity for legislatures to rally and drop their partisan stances to get legislation passed (Figure 9.2).

However, the gaps in the law that took place between the Food and Drug Administration Modernization Act of 1997 and the Drug Quality and Security Act of 2013 were known for years (503A and 503B). It may

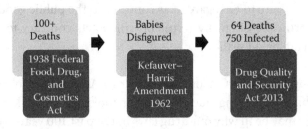

FIGURE 9.1
Driving forces behind major FDA legislation.

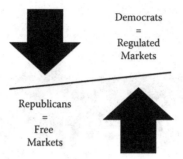

Democrats
=
Regulated
Markets

Republicans
=
Free
Markets

FIGURE 9.2
Political balancing act.

be wishful thinking, but there needs to be a preventive mindset with our lawmakers without overregulation that allows for common sense to address issues with existing laws. Earlier I mentioned the lawmaking process as making sausage. There is still room for common sense when the lives and health of our citizens are at stake. We must also allow room for common sense and not overregulate, chasing companies out of business and creating real drug shortages. Significant people will be affected if this happens—unintended consequences for using a sledge hammer instead of a paper clip!

INNOVATION

Our country has been blessed with a culture of innovation that exists in both private industry and the Food and Drug Administration (FDA) and other government agencies. We discussed in our introduction some of the discoveries to eradicate diseases, such as polio vaccines and penicillin, and lengthen our life spans. Sometimes the innovations are simple, yet effective. For example, the Professional Compounding Centers of America (PCCA) invented a lollipop with compounded medicines for people having difficulty swallowing. These people range from children having their tonsils out to adults with throat or esophagus cancer (see Figure 9.3).

We need to work with our representatives to push for public policy that rewards—and not retards—innovation. This may be a mix of private and public incentives. It also includes legislation to protect a strong return on the investment by pharmaceutical drug supply chain participants to enable strong R&D departments. We also need to identify and champion

FIGURE 9.3
PCCA lollipops with compounded medicines. (From PCCA. With permission.)

the "captains of our pharmaceutical drug supply chain." In Chapter 10, we review selected people who, in the past, have combined a vision for what's needed with innovative actions to make a difference.

DRUG SHORTAGES

Poor public policy (or at least one that is reactionary) and excessive regulations have the potential to create drug shortages. Under Title I of the Drug Quality and Security Act, the definition of a *compounding manufacturer* versus a *compounding pharmacy* has the potential to be very problematic. As we mentioned before, there are a significant number of small to medium compounding pharmacies that produce compounded medicines "for office use" for hospitals and medical facilities with patients that have physician prescriptions. I have heard several times from owners of compounding pharmacies that they spend a significant portion of their discretionary income on compliance to regulation activities, including lawyers, instead of additional capacity to compound medicines. There is a real possibility that if they are deemed manufacturers and subject to the current good manufacturing practices (cGMP), they will exit the business and shutter their capacity. Patients who rely on their compounded medicines will have to wait for their medicines or stand in a line for rationed supplies. Another big reason is the cost of litigation when mistakes are made. The more regulation, the greater the cost of litigation and risk mitigation.

FASTER FDA TRIALS AND DRUG SHORTAGES

The FDA must be commended for having a disciplined process to test pharmaceutical drugs and have them go on clinical trials before approving them. We certainly need to protect public safety and, as a practice, not rush approvals of pharmaceutical drugs. However, there are two areas that need to be improved and addressed with FDA trials.

We need a faster process to get needed medicines to patients. I am not a doctor or a scientist, but we need to review the process to accelerate time to approval without sacrificing drug safety. Patients in need are going without medicines while trials take place. In some cases, patients go abroad where medicines in an FDA trial are already available. In other cases, they join the trials. In way too many cases, they just go without and suffer the consequences. Fifteen years ago, my dad (Fred T. Kuglin) had macrodegenerative disease. There were medications and a surgery under review/trial (the implantation of a telescopic lens) that would slow the disease and preserve most of the eyesight for patients. By the time the medications and surgery were approved, my dad had lost most of his eyesight. My dad had numerous medical issues, and ultimately died of old age (87). However, he would lament that no matter what illness he battled, his quality of life was impacted most by his loss of eyesight. He would have benefitted from a faster FDA trial process. I wonder how many other "Fred T. Kuglins" across the spectrum of pharmaceutical drugs under FDA trials would ultimately benefit from a faster FDA trial process.

EBOLA, FDA TRIALS, AND PUBLIC POLICY

There is an excellent example going on right now where public policy and FDA trials cross paths with a potential epidemic. The following are key facts from the World Health Organization (WHO) on Ebola:

- The Ebola virus disease (EVD), formerly known as Ebola hemorrhagic fever, is a severe, often fatal illness in humans.
- The virus is transmitted to people from wild animals and spreads in the human population through human-to-human transmission.

- The average EVD case fatality rate is around 50%. Case fatality rates have varied from 25% to 90% in past outbreaks.
- The first EVD outbreaks occurred in remote villages in Central Africa, near tropical rain forests, but the most recent outbreak in West Africa has involved major urban as well as rural areas.
- Community engagement is key to successfully controlling outbreaks. Good outbreak control relies on applying a package of interventions, namely, case management, surveillance and contact tracing, a good laboratory service, safe burials, and social mobilization.
- Early supportive care with rehydration and symptomatic treatment improves survival. There is as yet no licensed treatment proven to neutralize the virus, but a range of blood, immunological, and drug therapies are under development.
- There are currently no licensed Ebola vaccines, but two potential candidates are undergoing evaluation.[3]

There are several items of note here. The first is the last bullet. The two potential Ebola vaccines undergoing evaluation have been "under evaluation" for years. With a mortality rate so high, why not immediately release them for use with the numerous people (here in the United States and in West Africa) with the hopes of increasing the recovery rates? Second is public policy around community engagement. One of the interventions mentioned in the bullet above is a quarantine of people who have come into close contact with an Ebola-stricken patient. Several countries demand quarantine periods for doctors, nurses, and loved ones who have come into contact with Ebola-stricken patients. We have multiple states that require different but stringent quarantine conditions (New York, New Jersey, Texas, etc.), an administration that pushes for loose restrictions, and our military that requires mandatory quarantine of all personnel that come back from West Africa.[4] Right now the belief is that we have hospitals with emergency room (ER) nurses and doctors that are ill-informed and ill-equipped to properly handle Ebola patients as they walk in for treatment. The Centers for Disease Control and Prevention (CDC) seems at odds with the WHO as well. *Where is the coordinated public policy to address this issue?* It seems that politics have intervened and common sense has taken a back seat. The bottom line is that we need the Ebola vaccines undergoing evaluation now to help save lives and a strong quarantine period for everyone exposed to Ebola. We also need our legislatures to work together, forget politics, and formulate public policy to protect everyone.

PHARMACEUTICAL DRUG COMPANIES
AND THE DRUG QUALITY AND SECURITY ACT

It is Chapter 9, and my readers are probably wondering, "Where are the pharmaceutical drug companies?" For Title I and drug compounding, there is limited exposure and participation with the pharmaceutical drug manufacturers unless they manufacture ingredients and fine chemicals. The pharmaceutical manufacturers do have to be careful not to allow drug products approved overseas but not yet approved in the United States to be imported into the United States through either direct importation or drug compounding and compounding pharmacies.

For Title II, virtually all the pharmaceutical drug manufacturers have antidiversion and anticounterfeiting divisions and activities. Johnson & Johnson has its active Anti-Counterfeiting Division.[5] Pfizer works closely with the FDA and other regulatory authorities to ensure that pharmaceutical companies have the resources they need to implement the anticounterfeiting technologies that work most effectively for their products. Pfizer is working collaboratively with wholesale distributors, pharmacies, Customs and Border Protection offices, and law enforcement agencies to increase inspections, monitor distribution channels, and improve surveillance of distributors and repackagers.[6] GlaxoSmithKline has an active anticounterfeiting program, which ranges from covert and overt markers on its packages to contract demands that only GSK products be purchased from GSK.[7] The list goes on and on.

Pharmaceutical drug manufacturers focus their efforts on the packaging and serialization of their products. From a drug quality standpoint, they want to make sure that when a patient takes one of their medicines, it is in fact one of their medicines. From a drug security standpoint, diversion, adulteration, and counterfeiting strike at the heart of their business—brand equity and the protection of their brand's value. If you ask any investment advisor about a pharmaceutical drug stock, the first thing the advisor will look for is its brand portfolio. The pharmaceutical drug manufacturers spend a huge amount of money in research and development (R&D) to develop their brands. From both risk mitigation and the protection of their brand assets, they have a heightened interest to work with the supply chain participants to eliminate diversion, adulteration, and counterfeiting. The reality is they can only do so much. The risk essentially starts as they "hand off" the pharmaceutical drugs at their shipping dock of the manufacturing plant to a carrier to go to a wholesale distributor.

TRUCKING COMPANIES AND THE DRUG QUALITY AND SECURITY ACT

We reviewed Title II and carriers in Chapter 6 when we discussed Internet pharmacies. However, it has been our experience that theft involving trucking companies has a wide range of perpetrators. There is the simple tampering of products (one box here, another there) that is difficult to detect and catch unless it is done over a sustained period of time. Then there is the intermediate level of theft. On July 23, 2014, a truck carrying $2 million worth of pharmaceutical drugs and narcotics (controlled substances) was stolen from a Bartow County, Georgia, truck stop. The driver left the truck running and unlocked while he ran into the truck stop to go to the bathroom. (This sounds unsafe, but it is a common practice for truck drivers not stopping for food and fuel, but only for the bathroom.) This had to be an inside job, according to reports. The perpetrators took the tractor trailer and even switched tractors within a short distance. Unfortunately for them, the tracking device was on the trailer![8]

One anonymous law enforcement official enlightened me during a lengthy conversation on theft of in-transit pharmaceutical drugs and controlled substances. He described a sophisticated and dangerous twist to the above truck heist scenario. Select people know what shipments of what products go on what trailers. These people include the pharmaceutical drug manufacturing plant, the trucking company assigned to pick up a shipment, and the destination personnel—more than likely the wholesale distributor. The intent of the above theft was to steal the pharmaceutical drugs and narcotics. The law enforcement official told me that organized crime groups have set up prototype packaging lines to produce products and packaging that looks almost identical to the pharmaceutical drug manufacturer's packaging. They also have people on the inside to share this shipment information. When the tractor trailer is "hijacked," it is taken to a nearby location where the cargo is switched out with the counterfeit product. Law enforcement personnel locate the hijacked trailers within, on average, 30 minutes (thanks to the trailer-tracking sensors). They look in the trailer and see the cargo as "present and untouched."

The appearance is that the thieves became "spooked" and just abandoned the pharmaceutical drugs and narcotics. The reality is that by the time the recovered drugs are tested for authenticity, the real drugs and narcotics are long gone. (Remember my Authentix example in Chapter 4? This is a perfect application of its markers and services.)

The real danger is that the recovered drugs and narcotics do not go through a strenuous testing for authenticity. People relying on these medicines could be harmed if they take the counterfeit drugs and narcotics. The pharmaceutical manufacturers are also harmed because the real drugs and narcotics will show up somewhere, either back into the forward supply chain or on the street corners. The loss of revenue can be far exceeded by the negative impact on brand value if something bad happens to patients as a result of the theft.

My anonymous law enforcement official gave me another scenario. The organized crime groups he refers to are duplicating trucks to look virtually identical to those of UPS, FedEx, and other carriers. These fake trucks have been cited going back and forth across the border from Texas and Arizona, transporting drugs, guns, and money. These trucks show up for pickups at the pharmaceutical drug manufacturing site on time, and leave with the pharmaceutical drug and narcotics shipments. The drivers have uniforms identical to the real ones. The drivers know the time, place, destination, and all other pertinent shipment information. The real pickup truck is somehow delayed. When it shows up, the pharmaceutical manufacturer knows that the theft just took place. These organized crime groups buy used trucks from the trucking companies through a broker, and then repaint them to look just like the originals. Talk about sophisticated theft with inside information!

ONE BARRIER BETWEEN PATIENTS AND ADULTERATED AND COUNTERFEIT DRUGS: NURSES

As pharmaceutical drug companies increase the number and types of drugs for patients, nurses have a growing role with patient safety. One leading doctor told me that nurses have become the front line for pharmaceutical drug safety in hospitals and medical facilities. I know that when I was in the hospital recovery room after my neck surgery, it was always the nurses testing my pain and administering my drugs. Nurses can sense adverse effects quickly, and can take appropriate action when they do occur. There is a growing need for "drug safety nurses." A quick check of nursing positions in demand showed drug safety nurses close to the top of the list.

There is another reason that nurses are becoming the front line for pharmaceutical drug safety in hospitals and medical facilities. Many hospitals and medical facilities have outsourced their pharmaceutical drug supply deliveries. These deliveries at times come right into the hospital and to the nurses' station on selected floors. The drugs are placed into the final inventory location where nurses get the drugs for their patients. With experience, nurses can potentially detect counterfeit or adulterated drugs before they are administered. They can also detect adverse effects immediately after counterfeit or adulterated drugs are administered. Any adverse reporting of the "proscribed drugs" starts with the nurse.

Another doctor, this one in a heart hospital, told me that nurses are relied on very heavily for reporting purposes for pharmaceutical drugs that are in clinical trials. I can believe this, because nurses have to have the trifecta of skills: knowledge of the disease being treated, knowledge of the pharmaceutical drug being administered, and the ability to communicate with the patient in "normal everyday language."

The bottom line is that nurses need several items to do their job with pharmaceutical drugs. First, they need a prescription or pharmaceutical drug order from a doctor. They also need the correct dosage delivered to them by the pharmacist (or picked up at the nurses' station). Nurses also need access to the correct drug information. This information is usually provided by the pharmacist. Additionally, nurses need training on the proper technique by which to administer the pharmaceutical drugs and how to report adverse situations. From compounded drugs to pharmaceutical drugs, nurses need these items to effectively fill their frontline drug quality and drug security roles.

SUMMARY—TITLE I: COMPOUNDING QUALITY ACT

Title I of the Drug Quality and Security Act of 2013 is called the Compounding Quality Act. It is a well-put-together law, intended to close gaps left over from the FDA Modernization Act of 1997 and address the issues responsible for the NECC fungal meningitis outbreak in 2012.

The FDA has taken several actions to implement the Compounding Quality Act. These actions include outsourcing facility registration and reporting, defining the conditions for traditional compounders not registered as outsourcing facilities to meet to qualify for the exemptions in Section 503A, and enhancing its communications with the states when concerns or actions are taken against compounding pharmacies acting contrary to Section 503A. It also includes the creation of a pharmacy compounding advisory committee before issuing certain regulations required by the law. This is a very positive action to help prevent laws that will be so strict as to cause compounding drug shortages. The FDA is required under Sections 503A and 503B to develop a list of drugs that may or may not be compounded and a list of bulk drug substances or ingredients that may be used to compound. Last, the FDA intends to continue proactive and for-cause inspections of compounding pharmacies and to take aggressive action, including enforcement actions, as appropriate, to protect the public health.[9]

There are a number of questions that still need to be answered, and many regulations that the FDA still needs to develop. At the top of the list is the gray area between a compound manufacturer and a traditional compounding pharmacy. It may be black and white to some legislatures and government officials, but there are a number of compounding pharmacies producing needed medicines for patients in this gray area. The subject of inspections is another area that can be a cause for confusion and conflict with states. We discussed the opportunity for an accredited firm to do proactive inspections based on FDA and state boards of pharmacy audits for compounding manufacturers and traditional compounding pharmacies. This service would go a long way to bridge the gap between the FDA and the state boards of pharmacy in terms of audits, focusing their energies on the offenders, not the entire compounding industry participants.

The issue of FDA trials for new drugs is only loosely connected to Title I, but it does need to be reviewed. Speed is of the essence with some life-saving medicines, and the process is entirely too long. The FDA should develop a separate advisory committee on how to cut the FDA trials' timeline in half, while reducing the risk to patients to dangerous side effects. Another unintended consequence of long FDA trials for new drugs is corruption. The more money that pharmaceutical drug companies invest in a new drug, the greater the chance that people involved in the FDA trial will be pressured to not report adverse conditions that result from using the drugs. I know my dad would have sacrificed the little sight he had left in his last few years to go through the trial or have access to the medicines that had the promise to improve his eyesight. Patients today must be clinically perfect candidates for FDA trial medicines to boost the overall results. My suggestion is to make these medicines available to people who might be high risk but have nothing to lose (Ebola patients and others).

Also, during my research for the book, many compounders are actually pharmacists that happen to own companies. Over time, many of these compounders have obtained multiple compounding sites, and face issues that are a mix of business, pharmaceutical compounding, and compliance issues. It is my recommendation that the National Association of Boards of Pharmacy (NABP) work with the FDA and state boards of pharmacy members to develop programs for the owners of compounding facilities that center on governance, leadership, and compliance with FDA regulations. This would help the owners feel less threatened by the new regulations, and enhance their effectiveness in balancing the production of safe compounded drugs for patients and operating a business that produces a return on the owner's investment.

SUMMARY—TITLE II: DRUG SUPPLY CHAIN SECURITY ACT

Title II of the Drug Quality and Security Act is called the Drug Supply Chain Security Act. Many insiders call it the Track and Trace Act. The objective of Title II is to facilitate the exchange of information at the individual package level about where a pharmaceutical drug has been in the supply chain. The law requires the FDA, within 10 years of November 27, 2013, to accomplish the following: enable verification of the legitimacy of the drug product identifier down to the package level, enhance detection and notification of illegitimate products in the drug supply chain, and facilitate more efficient recalls of drug products.

The FDA is already working with pharmaceutical drug manufacturers, wholesale distributors, repackagers, and pharmacies to develop a new system. This new system will include product identifiers, product tracing, product verification, detection and response procedures to quarantine and investigate suspect pharmaceutical drugs, and notification procedures (FDA and other stakeholders) when illegitimate drugs are found. Title II also includes provisions for wholesale distributors to report their licensing statuses and contact information to the FDA (good move), and for third-party logistics providers handling pharmaceutical drugs to obtain a state or federal license (even better move).[10]

In all honesty, I really do like Michael J. Fox and the *Back to the Future* movies. However, I hope this new system is not a "back-to-the-future effort" to the ePedigree of a few years ago. The dream of big iron companies (with numerous consultants cheering them on) was to develop a massive centralized database to enable track and trace for all pharmaceutical drugs. It was not practical for many reasons, including privacy and financial reasons. My hope is that the FDA's system embraces distributed computing with the supply chain participants, and avoids the push to develop an Affordable Care Act centralized system, which was such a disaster.

Care must be taken to work very closely with the wholesale distributors, and especially the big three, to design and implement regulations that work without disrupting the flow of pharmaceutical drugs. It is more critical for the FDA to design and implement regulations that do not materially harm wholesale distributors. Their profit margins are so thin that any adverse financial impact could cause a big supply disruption to pharmacies and patients. The wholesale distributors also play a key role with repackaging product for hospitals.

All supply chain participants play key roles in the effort to combat illegal Internet pharmacies and pill mills. All parties must be vigilant to identify and report pharmaceutical drugs that have been altered, stolen, diverted, or substituted with illegitimate product. The FDA needs to elevate the role of returns distributors in the effort to identify why product ends up in the pharmaceutical drug graveyard. The returns distributors have a wealth of information for pharmaceutical drug supply chain participants as well as state and federal law enforcement agencies. There is a huge opportunity for pharmaceutical drug companies to harness the why behind pharmaceutical drug returns, and translate this why into corrective action in their procurement and manufacturing processes. The Title II provisions around product identifiers and product tracing have the unintended benefit of helping pharmaceutical drug companies unlock this latent value opportunity.

One big unintended benefit of Title II is the use of product identifiers with state-of-the-art supply chain software systems to track supply throughout the supply chain and match the supply to actual demand. At first this will probably happen with the fastest-moving and highest-value pharmaceutical drugs. Pharmaceutical drug manufacturers will have to work with wholesale distributors and major retail pharmacy chains to do this on an integrated basis. In a controlled environment, there is also a real application with controlled substances—in close collaboration with the DEA. By compressing supply with demand, inventory turns will increase, enhancing free cash flow and reducing unsaleable returns. By closely tracking supply to demand, the process for recalls and quarantine of suspect pharmaceutical drugs becomes faster, easier, and more accurate.

Another big unintended benefit from the Title II regulations is the possibility of reducing returns by understanding the why behind the returns. Understanding why returns occur can lead to changes in policies and procedures for the procurement and manufacturing processes with pharmaceutical drug manufacturers. The efficiencies gained in the forward supply chain have the potential to far outstrip the reduction in returns.

CONCLUSION

Our hearts and prayers go out to the families of the 64 people who died and the 751 people with fungal infections from tainted medicine produced by the NECC.[11] The Drug Quality and Security Act became law to address the legislative and oversight deficiencies that allowed the tainted medicine to be given to patients. While the law is not perfect (and not quite finished), as we pointed out throughout the book, it is a big step forward to protecting patients in need of compounded medications. My hat is off to the 99% of the pharmaceutical drug supply chain workers who day by day and hour by hour work so hard to protect our drug quality and drug security, as well as our fine law enforcement personnel who deal with the 1%. The journey continues!

ENDNOTES

1. http://www.merriam-webster.com/dictionary/public%20policy.
2. http://www.fda.com; input from John Swann, FDA historian, October 2014.
3. Ebola Virus Disease, WHO, http://www.who.int/mediacentre/factsheets/fs103/en/.
4. Fog of Ebola War: White House Stance Unclear as Military Leaders Urge U.S. Troop Quarantine, *Fox News*, 2014, http://www.foxnews.com/politics/2014/10/27/joint-chiefs-call-for-quarantine-troops-returning-from-ebola-zone/.
5. http://www.jnj.com/.

6. Counterfeiting & Importation, Pfizer, http://www.pfizer.com/products/counterfeit_ and_importation/counterfeit_importation.

7. GlaxoSmithKline Supports FDA Efforts to Protect against Counterfeit Drugs, PR Newswire, http://www.prnewswire.com/news-releases/glaxosmithkline-supports-fda-efforts-to-protect-against-counterfeit-drugs-71695472.html.

8. Tom Regan, Thieves Steal Truck Filled with $2 Million Worth of Pharmaceutical Drugs, Cargo Security Alliance, 2014, https://www.securecargo.org/news/thieves-steal-truck-filled-with-2-million-worth-of-pharmaceutical-drugs.

9. Compounding, FDA, http://www.fda.gov/drugs/GuidanceComplianceRegulatory Information/Pharmacy Compounding/.

10. Drug Supply Chain Security Act (DSCSA), FDA, http://www.fda.gov/Drugs/ DrugSafety/DrugIntegrityandSupplyChainSecurity/DrugSupplyChainSecurityAct/.

11. Multistate Outbreak of Fungal Meningitis and Other Infections—Case Count, CDC, http://www.cdc.gov/hai/outbreaks/meningitis-map-large.html.

10

Drug Quality and Security Hall of Fame

INTRODUCTION

There have been numerous people who have significantly contributed to drug quality and drug security throughout history. It is impossible to pay tribute to everyone, from leaders of countries and legislators to research specialists, from pharmacists to emergency room nurses and law enforcement personnel, and from wholesale distributor repackaging specialists to receiving supervisors of returns logistics providers. During my research for this book, there are a few that stand out that I would like to showcase for my readers. I do this with hope that others will be inspired to be the next-generation "hall of fame" members in drug quality and drug security.

DAVID SPARKS, FOUNDER OF PCCA

L. David Sparks worked for 22 years as the owner/pharmacist of independent pharmacies in the Tulsa, Oklahoma, area (Figure 10.1). He was instrumental in introducing the compounding pharmacy to the hospice environment. He helped establish the Oklahoma Hospice Organization and was a founding director of the Hospice of Green Country in Oklahoma. According to his official bio, David deeply believes that pharmacy compounding is necessary for meeting patients' medical challenges.

FIGURE 10.1
David Sparks. (From PCCA. With permission.)

David moved to Texas in 1988, and in 1991 became CEO and in 1992 president of the Professional Compounding Centers of America (PCCA). In 2003, David helped to found Eagle Analytical Services. David has a passion for teaching. Every year, pharmacists, pharmacy technicians, and college pharmacy students attend PCCA's compounding training classes, which are taught according to U.S. Pharmacopeia (USP) 795 and 797 guidelines. Participants learn to compound formulations, including gels, lip balms, topicals, suppositories, and capsules, in PCCA's in-house training laboratory. They also attend classroom lectures, covering a variety of topics, such as quality assurance, legal issues, and marketing. In 1999, under David's leadership, PCCA received Texas Pharmacy Association's Excellence in Corporate Education award.

Over the past several years, Mr. Sparks has led the effort to preserve pharmacists' right to compound, and was instrumental, along with several other pharmacy organizations, in obtaining passage of the FDA Modernization Act of 1997 and the inclusion of Section 503A (see Chapters 2 and 8). Section 503A was critical because it ensured that compounding pharmacists have the ability to compound and preserves the critical triad relationship of the patient, physician, and pharmacist.

What really impressed me about David was his culture and passion for quality control. Today's leaders at PCCA have adopted David's culture and passion for quality control, making PCCA a beacon for pharmaceutical compounding drug quality and security.[1]

FIGURE 10.2
Colonel Eli Lilly. (From Eli Lilly and Company. With permission.)

THE ELI LILLY FAMILY

Eli Lilly and Company was founded in May 1876 by Colonel Eli Lilly in Indianapolis, Indiana, where its headquarters exists today (Figure 10.2). At the time, Colonel Lilly was a pharmaceutical chemist and a veteran of the U.S. Civil War. He was frustrated by the poorly prepared, often ineffective medicines of his day. Consequently, he made these commitments to himself and society:

- He would found a company that manufactured pharmaceutical products of the highest possible quality.
- His company would develop only medicines that would be dispensed at the suggestion of physicians, rather than by eloquent sideshow hucksters.
- Lilly pharmaceuticals would be based on the best science of the day.

Colonel Lilly laid the foundation for the Lilly tradition: a dedication that first concentrated on the quality of existing products and later expanded to include the discovery and development of new and better pharmaceuticals. All of this was incredible, because it would take until 1907 to pass the Wiley Act.

FIGURE 10.3
J.K. Lilly, Sr. (From Eli Lilly and Company. With permission.)

Colonel Lilly's son, Josiah K. Lilly Sr., succeeded Colonel Lilly as president of the company (Figure 10.3). He started with Eli Lilly Company in June 1876 as "porter, engineer, miller, mass maker, bottle washer, errand boy and general utility man." By 1898, he became president of Eli Lilly, a position he would hold for 34 years. Eli Lilly Company grew despite recessionary periods under his direction. However, he is known for his groundbreaking efforts through a partnership with Connaught Antitoxin Laboratories to lay the groundwork to mass produce insulin.

Colonel Lilly's grandson, Eli Lilly, became the company's third president, and would lead the company from 1932 to 1948 (Figure 10.4). Under

FIGURE 10.4
Eli Lilly. (From Eli Lilly and Company. With permission.)

FIGURE 10.5
J.K. Lilly, Jr. (From Eli Lilly and Company. With permission.)

Eli's leadership, the company expanded operations in Indianapolis and overseas, and established a reputation as a good place to work. During World War II, the company supported the war effort by producing blood plasma in conjunction with the American Red Cross. It also manufactured encephalitis vaccine, antitoxin for gas poisoning, vaccines for flu and typhus, as well as insulin, Merthiolate, and other drugs. Lilly was especially proud of the company's collaboration with the U.S. government and others on large-scale production of penicillin.

Josiah K. Lilly Jr., the son of Josiah K. Lilly Sr. and grandson of Colonel Lilly, served as president of the company from 1948 to 1953 (Figure 10.5). He was the last Lilly to serve as president.

All four contributed distinctive approaches to management and a passion for philanthropy. Together, these management styles established a corporate culture in which Lilly employees were viewed as the company's most valuable assets, drug quality was of highest importance, and the company was driven to discover important medical breakthroughs. Their leadership steered the company through recessions, the Great Depression, and two world wars. Today Eli Lilly and Company has pharmaceutical drugs in the oncology, cardiovascular, diabetes, critical care, neuroscience, men's health, and musculoskeletal fields. The company has an active anti-counterfeiting program that includes serialization, diversion control, and educational activities to identify the roles of Eli Lilly, the patient, and the government. The Lilly family no longer is at the helm as president, but their legacy lives on in pursuit of drug quality and drug security.[2]

JOHN MCKESSON, FOUNDER, NEIL E. HARMON AND ALAN SEELENFREUND, CEOS, MCKESSON AND COMPANY

In Chapter 5, we covered the history of McKesson with John McKesson and Charles Olcott starting the company in 1833. In 1853, two years before the death of Charles Olcott, Daniel Robbins became John McKesson's partner and the company was renamed McKesson & Robbins. John McKesson passed away in 1893, 50 years after his founding of McKesson. Not much is known about John McKesson's life, but he did start a wholesale drug and import company that lasted 50 years and spanned the Civil War and the financial capitalist era. Little would he know that the company he started would still be in existence today (Figure 10.6).

From my research, Neil E. Harlan was not only a very smart man, but also a beloved leader of McKesson during turbulent times. He received an undergraduate degree from Arkansas and both an MBA and DBA in business from Harvard University Graduate School of Business Administration. Mr. Harlan proudly served his country in the U.S. Army during World War II. In 1951, Mr. Harlan was appointed to the faculty of the Harvard Business School where he served as full professor until 1962, when he was appointed the assistant secretary of the Air Force by President John F. Kennedy. From 1964 until 1967 he worked at Anderson, Clayton & Company, Houston, Texas, in positions including financial vice

FIGURE 10.6
John McKesson. (From McKesson. With permission.)

president, executive vice president, and member of the board of directors. From 1967 until 1974 he was a director of McKinsey & Company. And from 1974 until 1993, Mr. Harlan was with McKesson Corporation serving as chairman, president and chief executive officer, director, and finally interim chairman and CEO.

During his tenure at McKesson, Neil Harlan led McKesson on a transition to focus on health care and divest unrelated businesses. He also focused McKesson's resources on automation and services within health care. Throughout the 20 years he served as McKesson's leader, the company steadily increased its focus on the wholesale distribution of pharmaceutical drugs as the cornerstone of its health care services portfolio.

Working in tandem with Neil Harlan was Alan Seelenfreund. Alan Seelenfreund stated with McKesson in 1975. He became chief financial officer in 1984 and joined the McKesson board in 1988. In 1989, he was elected chairman and chief executive officer, the latter a position he held until April 1997. Investors often point to the Harlan/Seelenfreund years as the formative years for McKesson, focusing on health care and growing, by acquisitions and securing large customers such as Walmart in 1989.

John McKesson founded McKesson and Company and led it for its first 60 years. Neil Harlan led McKesson for 20+ years with Alan Seelenfreund, and sharpened the focus of the company on the very services that anchor the company today. Without these three individuals, McKesson would probably not be the largest and most profitable wholesale distribution company in the pharmaceutical drug industry.[3]

HERB SHEER: GENCO—THIRD GENERATION

When I started doing investigative research for this book, I visited numerous pharmacy retailers. What I discovered was that one company, GENCO, seemed to hold the largest market share in the pharmaceutical drug returns industry. In addition, I heard comments such as "innovators" and "value-added providers" when GENCO's name came up. This was intriguing, since my son and coauthor, Karl, worked for Inmar and the industry is known for being obsessive with cost cutting. What I discovered is that the passion for reverse logistics and the strong culture could be traced to the Sheer family, specifically Herb Sheer (Figure 10.7).

FIGURE 10.7
Herb Sheer. (From GENCO. With permission.)

Herb Sheer is the third-generation principal owner of GENCO, North America's recognized leader in Product Lifecycle Logistics˚ and a pioneer in reverse logistics. GENCO operates 140 value-added warehouse locations comprising 38 million square feet, manages $1.5 billion in freight, and liquidates over $2.5 billion in return product. GENCO's diverse range of customers includes many Fortune 500 companies in the technology, consumer, industrial, retail, and health care markets and the federal government. GENCO's complete range of product life cycle services include inbound logistics; warehousing and distribution; fulfillment; contract packaging and managed transportation; systems integration; returns processing and disposition; test, repair, and refurbishment; product liquidation; and recycling.

Herb joined GENCO in 1971 following in the footsteps of his father and grandfather, who founded the company in 1898, and became executive chairman in 2013. Herb is a supply chain innovator. He founded the centralized returns process known today as reverse logistics out of necessity and opportunity. He saw that returned products were oftentimes unwanted and destined for the landfill. In essence, Herb believed in sustainability before it was the cool thing to do. He understood the challenges of inventory management, the contractual relationships between manufacturers and retailers, and the value of returned products and knew that technology was the key. GENCO developed a proprietary software system that manages returned product with the various disposition channels while providing complete visibility to the inventory and the process. But Herb did not stop with reverse logistics. Just managing returns was only a half step. Herb understood that the market for selling returned product lacked transparency and scale, and he entered the liquidation or remarketing industry in 1992. Herb's latest passion in the supply chain is automation technology and robotics. From automated guided vehicles (AGVs) to new ways to manage process within the four walls, Herb never stops innovating.

Over the course of Herb's 40+-year career at GENCO, he has made numerous acquisitions to grow the company and add new services. From Cumberland Distribution in 1999, IOgistics in 2003, and Capital Returns in 2005 to the $512 million acquisition of ATC Technology Corporation in 2010, Herb has transformed GENCO into a $1.5 billion third-party logistics provider with an impressive roster of Fortune 500 customers across the United States, Canada, Mexico, and the Middle East.

Herb is a past recipient of the Council of Supply Chain Management Professionals' Distinguished Service Award, the association's highest honor; the Syracuse University Martin J. Whitman School of Management's Salzberg Medallion; and the first recipient of the Reverse Logistics Association's Lifetime Achievement Award. Herb's contributions to reverse logistics and his pursuit of excellence with the pharmaceutical returns process position GENCO as the leader in pharmaceutical drug returns.[4]

DR. HARVEY W. WILEY, FDA

Dr. Wiley began his government career in 1882 as chief chemist with the U.S. Department of Agriculture (Figure 10.8). He had a solid understanding of agriculture with an empathetic approach to the agriculture industry and its problems. He also demonstrated a talent for public relations.

Dr. Wiley would spend his initial years pursuing the safety of chemical preservatives being used in foods. In 1902, he was appropriated $5,000 to study the effects of various chemical preservatives on human volunteers. This study's research team was nicknamed "The Poison Squad," and would draw national attention. Ultimately, this attention would shift to the need for a federal food and drug law. Dr. Wiley soon put his public relations skills to work and become the main sponsor and spokesman for national

FIGURE 10.8
Portrait of Dr. Harvey W. Wiley. (From Kristofer Baumgartner, CDER Trade Press, FDA. With permission.)

food and drug regulation. He worked with a woman named Alice Lakey, and succeeded in getting over 1 million women to write to the White House in support of his proposed national food and drug regulation. (This was enormous accomplishment at the time without the Internet!)

The Pure Food and Drugs Act would ultimately pass in 1906, and Dr. Wiley was honored with the act's nickname, the Wiley Act. The enforcement of the Wiley Act was given to the Bureau of Chemistry, another tribute to Dr. Wiley and the efforts of the Bureau of Chemistry in studying food and drug adulteration and misbranding. One of his main accomplishments after the Wiley Act was the development for standards for truth in labeling. The lawsuit against the Coca-Cola Company in 1911 had two areas of contention. The first was that the name was "illegal" because there was no actual cocaine in its beverages. The second was that it contained caffeine as an additive without proper labeling. What resulted was the foundation for standards for truth in labeling for both food and pharmaceutical drugs.

In 1912, Dr. Wiley resigned to become the head of the Good Housekeeping laboratories. He remained with Good Housekeeping for 18 years until his death in 1930. He has had a postage stamp, a ship, several buildings, and a distinguished professor of chemistry position at Purdue University named after him. Perhaps the most prestigious honor is the Association of Official Agricultural Chemists (AOAC) top scientific award, instituted in 1956 and named after him.[5]

LEGISLATURE—FRED UPTON

As we mentioned in Chapter 1, Representative Fred Upton and his committee was instrumental in being the primary sponsor of H.R. 3204, which when signed into law became the Drug Quality and Security Act (Figure 10.9). Representative Fred Upton released this statement on November 27, 2013:

> With the President's signature today, this bipartisan law will help prevent future crises like last year's deadly fungal meningitis outbreak while also establishing a unified framework for maintaining safety throughout the drug supply chain. Across the nation, Americans going to their doctor's office or pharmacy will now have the confidence that their drugs are safe. From bipartisan oversight to drafting and approving legislation, we were able to reach a compromise to protect the drug supply and also remove regulatory roadblocks, creating an environment conducive to job creation. I am thankful for the cooperation of my colleagues in both the House and the Senate, on both sides of the aisle, for their efforts in this achievement.[6]

Representative Upton's accomplishment was even more noteworthy because of the partisan politics that have permeated two of the three branches of government since 2008.

Congressman Fred Upton represents a House district in southwest Michigan that stretches from the shores of Lake Michigan and includes key

FIGURE 10.9
Representative Fred Upton. (From the Office of Representative Fred Upton. With permission.)

industries that range from automobile parts manufacturing to high-tech biomedical innovation centers to agriculture.

Since 2011, Fred has served as chairman of the Committee on Energy and Commerce.

Prior to his election to Congress, Fred worked for President Ronald Reagan in the Office of Management and Budget (OMB). While at OMB, he learned from President Reagan's example that it does not matter who gets the credit, as long as the job gets done. That has been Fred's approach as chairman—every good idea is welcome, and the committee has plenty of bipartisan success to show for it.

For the committee, Fred is focused on three primary goals of promoting job creation and economic growth, transforming Washington to create a smaller, modernized government for the innovation era, and protecting families, communities, and civic initiatives.

The committee has built a significant record of results on public health issues. Among those achievements is legislation to advance research for children with rare and genetic diseases, strengthen the prescription drug supply chain in order to protect families against counterfeit drugs (Title II of the Drug Quality and Security Act), and streamline the federal approval process for new and generic drugs.

In 2014, Fred unveiled the bipartisan 21st Century Cures initiative, a multiyear effort that aims to accelerate the pace of cures and medical breakthroughs in the United States. The committee is taking a comprehensive look at the full arc of accelerating cures to help provide patients with better access to treatments and trials, and to ensure the United States maintains its leadership role in health research and care. As we discussed in Chapter 9, the need for faster FDA trials and streamlined processes for new drugs is very high.

Fred was born on April 23, 1953, and holds a bachelor's degree in journalism from the University of Michigan. He and his wife, Amey, have two children.[7]

DAVID JOSEPH BALLARD, CHIEF QUALITY OFFICER, BAYLOR SCOTT & WHITE HEALTH

When I first met David, we were on an airplane going to the East Coast and I had the pleasure of sitting next to him. It took maybe five minutes

FIGURE 10.10
Dr. David J. Ballard. (From Baylor Scott & White Health. With permission.)

before the subject of quality in health care delivery came up as a matter of conversation. At the time, I was doing strategic and operating plans for senior executives. In no time, David was the teacher and I was the student, eagerly listening to what the master had to say (Figure 10.10).

Toward the end of my time writing this book, I reached out to David to let him know of my topic and my thoughts on drug quality and drug security. He immediately "got it" and viewed the subject of my book (and the new Drug Quality and Security Act) from a three-dimensional health care delivery lens. David's approach starts with strong governance and leadership, and using these two as cornerstones, proceeds through the health care disciplines (oncology, cardiology, etc.). He told me that drug quality and drug security were an integral part of the delivery of health care, and permeated every phase. To David, it is all about the journey to health care quality improvement. This is exactly what everyone associated with the Drug Quality and Security Act hopes is the end game for the new law.

David was appointed on October 1, 2013, as the chief quality officer of Baylor Scott & White Health (BSWH), the largest not-for-profit health care system in Texas, which includes 43 hospitals, 500 patient care sites, 6,000 affiliated physicians, 36,000 employees, and the Scott & White health plan. A board-certified internist, he trained at the Mayo Graduate School of Medicine following completion of degrees in chemistry, economics, epidemiology, and medicine at the University of North Carolina (UNC), where he was a Morehead Scholar, North Carolina Fellow, and junior year Phi Beta Kappa inductee. David held progressive academic appointments as assistant and then associate professor at the Mayo Medical School, as associate professor with tenure at the University of Virginia School of Medicine, and as professor of medicine with tenure in the Emory University School of Medicine and professor of epidemiology in the Rollins School of Public Health of Emory University. He joined the Baylor Health Care System (BHCS) in 1999 as its first chief quality officer. He serves on the board of managers of the Heart Hospital Baylor Plano and the BHCS-Kessler/Select rehabilitation and long-term care joint venture. David also is a member of the executive committee of the High Value Healthcare Collaborative. BHCS has been recognized by many organizations for its health care improvement accomplishments under David's leadership, including the 2007 Leapfrog Patient-Centered Care Award, the 2008 National Quality Healthcare Award of the National Quality Forum, and the 2010 Medical Group Preeminence Award of the American Medical Group Association. In July 2011 David was appointed president of the BHCS (now BSWH) STEEEP Global Institute, which provides health care performance improvement solutions to health care organizations throughout the world. In 2012 David was selected as chair of the newly formed BHCS STEEEP Governance Council to set strategy and direction for operational functions related to STEEEP (safe, timely, effective, efficient, equitable, patient-centered) care across BHCS, which is now scaled across BSWH under David's leadership.

David serves on the editorial boards of *Health Services Research*, the *Journal of Comparative Effectiveness Research*, and the *Mayo Clinic Proceedings* (as health policy section editor). His book *Achieving STEEEP Health Care*, which was published in 2013, received the Shingo Research Award for its contributions to operational excellence and was followed by the publication of its companion book, *Guide to Achieving STEEEP Health Care*, at the end of 2014. I would need a couple more pages to detail all of his accomplishments and the boards he has served on or is currently serving on. David seems to have more degrees and prestigious awards than graduate courses I took to get my MBA![8]

More than anything, David has a passion for health care quality improvement and the people working in the health care industry. He understands drug quality and drug security, and hopes the new law is a positive step to improve the delivery of health care to patients in need. His accomplishments are many, but do not measure up to the impact he has had on the people he works with and, in this case, has met on an airplane.

SUMMARY

Throughout the book, we have cited numerous instances of people behaving badly. From the New England Compounding Center (NECC) and the fungal meningitis outbreak to the theft/diversion of pharmaceutical drugs, and from pill mills to illegal Internet pharmacies, there are bad people doing bad things in the pharmaceutical drug industry. With close to 2 million people employed throughout the supply chain, the 1% club amounts to a lot of bad people.

What is exhilarating about the people in my drug quality and drug security hall of fame is that they all had a vision and a passion to do the right things right for patients like you and me. Make no mistake about it, these people were also capitalists and knew how to make money. However, they accomplished so much and were ahead of their time in making money while doing the right things right. David Sparks founded PCCA with a focus on quality of ingredients and fine chemicals for compounding pharmacies, and lobbied Congress to put in protections for compounding pharmacies in the FDA Modernization Act of 1997. The Eli Lilly Family—Colonel Eli Lilly, J.K. Lilly Sr., Eli Lilly, and J.K. Lilly Jr.—led the Eli Lilly and Company from 1876 to 1953. They combined innovation with quality and making money with philanthropy. Their founding principles still exist today with the Eli Lilly Company, the Lilly Foundation, and the Lilly Endowment Fund. John McKesson founded McKesson before the Civil War, while Neil E. Harmon and Alan Seelenfreund would steer the company to what it is today—the largest wholesale distributor in the pharmaceutical drug industry and an early adopter of technology to enable its business. The vision and perseverance of all three men in two different centuries make the history of McKesson very rich.

Herb Sheer is the grandson of the founder of GENCO, and had the vision to move GENCO into the world of reverse logistics before reverse logistics was on anyone's radar screen. GENCO is not only a very large privately owned company, but it has the largest market share in returns logistics for pharmaceutical drugs. Dr. Harvey Wiley worked as a chemist for over 23 years, lobbying for the passage of the Wiley Act in 1906. He fought a lot of special interest groups to get the act passed. If you read his history (which I highly recommend), he paid a political price after the act was passed, with people trying to discredit his work. Throughout all of this, he persevered.

Representative Fred Upton initiated a committee and drove through a bipartisan bill (H.R. 3204) that would become the Drug Quality and Security Act of 2013. He did this in one of the most partisan Congresses that we have had in decades. He continues his work in this area, trying to streamline the FDA trials process to accelerate getting medicines to patients in need. Dr. David Ballard has an unbelievable passion and quest for continuous improvement in the quality of health care delivered to patients. His philosophy starts with governance and leadership, and permeates all the lines of business that exist in the delivery of health care to patients. Drug quality and drug security are a third dimension that fits into all stages of his model for health care delivery.

These people were remarkable. There are so many deserving people in the past 150+ years that one book couldn't possibly even list them if we had their names. They are an inspiration to all of us. I hope they inspire others to continue the journey and be the leaders of tomorrow in drug quality and drug security.

ENDNOTES

1. David Sparks bio, as provided by Aaron Lopez, PCCA, October 2014.
2. http://www.lilly.com/about/Pages/default.aspx; Michael Jarrell, historian/archivist, and Nola Heynes, library portfolio manager, Eli Lilly and Company, November 6, 2014.
3. http://www.mckesson.com/about-mckesson/our-history/; Kristin Hunter, senior manager, Corporate Media Relations, McKesson Corporation.
4. http://www.genco.com/About/history.php; Ryan Kelly, Senior VP Strategy and Marketing, GENCO, November 8, 2014.
5. Wallace F. Janssen, The Story of the Laws behind the Labels, *FDA Consumer*, 1981, http://www.fda.gov/AboutFDA/WhatWeDo/History/Overviews/ucm056044.htm; Kristofer Baumgartner, CDER Trade Press, Food and Drug Administration, with John Swann, FDA historian.
6. Upton Thankful as Pediatric Research, Meningitis/Drug Safety Bills Signed into Law, press release, 2013, http://upton.house.gov/news/documentsingle.aspx?DocumentID=363070.
7. Nicholas Culp, Office of Representative Fred Upton, November 19, 2014.
8. David Ballard, Chief Quality Officer, Baylor Scott & White Health, November 6 and 11, 2014.

Index

Printed in the United States
by Baker & Taylor Publisher Services

Printed in the United States
by Baker & Taylor Publisher Services